M Hamilton

Across an Ulster Bog

M Hamilton

Across an Ulster Bog

ISBN/EAN: 9783744691932

Printed in Europe, USA, Canada, Australia, Japan

Cover: Foto ©Thomas Meinert / pixelio.de

More available books at **www.hansebooks.com**

Across an Ulster Bog

By

M. Hamilton

Author of
"A Self-Denying Ordinance," etc.

London
William Heinemann
1896

Across an Ulster Bog

CHAPTER I

The rain was falling with a soft, persistent sound.

When Ellen went to the door to look out for her father, she could distinguish little save a brown blur of bog-land, with a grey, misty background. The dark pools of turf-water were full to overflowing, and the dripping rushes beside them bent and clung together; the cotton-grass, with all its fresh whiteness gone, was beaten down into the heather in pitiable, soiled masses. Near the lake, a straggling row of poplars stood out with ghostly indistinctness.

A sense of utter isolation weighed upon Ellen; the rain seemed to shut her out from human sight or sound, a solitary human creature. She knew that if the mist lifted she would be able to see the smoke from half-a-dozen chimneys across the bog, and as many distant groups coming back from their work along the damp road; but the knowledge only gave a background of relief to the strange, unreal feeling of aloneness.

She held the door open, that her father might see the light of the fire as he came across the bog. A few drops of rain drifted in and touched her hair, and she drew back a little farther into the shelter of the cottage.

Her work for the day was not very heavy, and she had finished it long ago. She had brought in both the goats, after her usual difficulties with the grey one, which was no respecter of persons, and butted at Ellen as readily as at any one else; she had fed the chickens on the potatoes left over after dinner, and brushed up the earth floor in the kitchen to leave no three-cornered marks of their wet little feet. Then, just after the rain had come on, she had made up a bright fire, put the kettle on to boil, and got everything ready for her father's tea.

Most of the live creatures had gone to bed early, in disgust with the weather. The old mother pig was still out for an airing; she was of an obstinate disposition, and did not allow her regular afternoon walk on the midden to be lightly interfered with. But her temper was ruffled, and she stopped to quarrel viciously with a couple of dissipated-looking chickens over a remnant of potato.

Ellen interfered and drove her back to her children, grunting ill-humouredly.

Inside the house a brown puppy and a couple of kittens were having it all to themselves, and were squabbling in a warm corner with small yelps and growls. The father's seat was ready for him—a wooden chair drawn in closely to the fire, where a brown tea-pot was warming in the ashes.

When Ellen caught sight of him, a shadowy figure drawing out of the mist, she went in to get his thick delf cup and saucer and little jug of goat's milk from the dresser.

Lindsay came in heavily, leaving a little pool behind him with every step. He was a tall man, and would have been taller but for a decided stoop of his shoulders. He had merry blue eyes, like his daughter's, in a face which would otherwise have been stern, with large features and high cheek-bones.

He drew a stool to the fire and began to unlace his wet boots.

"I'll hold you're ready for your tea, da," said Ellen; "it's a saft evening."

She had a pretty voice, with less than the usual tendency of her class to speak too loud, and a quick, gentle way of moving, which was peculiarly her own.

"Ay; it's terrible coorse," Lindsay said.

He was not a man of many words. He shook the rain from his coat, and warmed his hands over the fire in silence.

Ellen knelt down on the hearth and put on some more turf, with the puppy sprawling over her dress and biting at her bare feet, in imminent danger of getting burned. When it jumped up and caught her hair, she pushed it away and laughed.

"Quit, will you! Suchan a dog! It would take one to have nothing to do but to mind him. I have washed a bucketful of spuds for the dinner to-morrow, da. Would you like one to your tea?"

Lindsay shook his head. "I'll do rightly. Did you mind about changing the goat's straw in the byre?"

"Sure it's not much I forget. Is it, now?"

Lindsay kicked off his boots and put his feet to the fire with a sigh of satisfaction.

"We had to give over work a bit early," he said. "It's as well the rain held off so long, or it's a quare lint-pulling they'd have had at Dawson's. What kep' you from going up, daughter? You'll miss all the dancing and sport."

"I thought I would as lieve stop at home when it come to the time," said Ellen in a low voice. She knew that her father would be surprised. Dawson's lint-pulling was something looked forward to all through the year, next to, even if a long way after, the 12th of July. Last year she had talked about it for weeks before and months after.

"Why, what ails you, Ellen?" he said, as she knew he would say. "You're not overly fond of setting at home when there's sport going. I had a sight of them in the field, and there's fifty if there's one. They say there's foreigners from across the lake, and a wheen of boys out of Sloughan. I'm not willing for you to miss it. Clane yourself up, and I'll take you over when I've done my tea. We'll be there by six o'clock clever, and it's not as if Eccles and Wully weren't there to fetch you home."

"You're just going to set still and dry yourself," said Ellen, with a forced laugh. "I've no mind to go, and I wouldn't like to go for the dancin' when I'd worked none. And forby that, I've a sore head. Will I get your pipe?"

Lindsay said no more. Perhaps, being human, and exceedingly wet and reasonably tired, he was not particularly anxious to go out again.

Ellen brought him his pipe, and drew in a stool to the fire for herself. She sat with her elbows on her knees, watching the light flame with troubled eyes. She had something to say to her father, but she waited to say it till the dusk had drawn, so that he should not see her face.

A long silence fell between them. The rain drifted against the window; the clock ticked; some burnt-out turf fell together with a soft noise. Lindsay scarcely moved, except to knock the ashes out of his pipe, and the kittens had crawled into Ellen's lap and fallen asleep. Only the puppy was restless, and finding himself unnoticed, proceeded to amuse himself after his own fashion.

With much fuss and effort he dragged the cushion of a rough wooden arm-chair into the middle of the kitchen, and collected things from all parts of the room to put on the top—an apron of Ellen's, a long feather dropped by one of the hens, an old hat of Lindsay's, and some odd bits of newspaper. He proceeded with little runs and guilty pauses, marvelling at his impunity, and when he could find nothing more he collapsed into a fat, brown heap on the floor, panting and worn-out with his exertions.

Very gradually the tall, delf-filled dresser grew to a dim blur, and the blue check curtains of the bed which filled one corner became vague.

Ellen waited till the geraniums in the window were nothing but dark blots. Then she spoke, breaking the silence with an uncomfortable abruptness.

"Father, I've been wanting to ask you about letting me go to service."

Her father changed his position with a start and let his pipe drop. Her words came to him as a complete surprise. Six months ago there had been some question of sending her to Australia to her sisters, but he had entirely opposed it, and had hoped it was forgotten. Ellen was only sixteen, and she was more to him than all his other children put together.

He did not answer for a moment or two; he stooped with great deliberation to pick up his pipe, and drew several long whiffs. Then he looked across at his daughter; her head was bent, and he could only distinguish the thick plait of fair hair which lay down her back, and on which the firelight shone.

"What's been putting that in your head?" he said roughly.

"I've been thinking," said Ellen, with a little hurry in her voice, "that when Eccles marries—and if all the sough's true, it won't be long first—when Eccles marries, if he brings her here there'll be naught for two of us to do—I'd just be lossing myself. And what's the weaving now?—not worth keeping me at home to be winding bobbins for you. Mrs. Baring would likely find me a place."

Ellen spoke rather breathlessly; she had considered over and over again what she must say, and the words came like a lesson.

"I thought you were content enough here," Lindsay said. "Sure I've heard you say time and again that you wouldn't take any money and live anywhere else."

Ellen plaited her apron with her fingers, and kept her face turned away.

"But when Eccles marries there'll be naught for me to do."

"Sure, since the time Eccles was that height, he's always been after some girl or other, and never the same two weeks following other. And if he was married there's no call for him to bring her here. You're better at home, daughter."

Ellen gave a long sigh.

"But if you're set on it—and there was a place near hand. But I wouldn't let you go for the next year or two, till you are come to your strength. And I'd be loath enough to part wi' you then, while I'm fit to keep you at home."

Ellen made no answer. Sheltered by the dusk, she sat looking straight before her with unseeing eyes.

There was nothing more to be said; her father's words were entirely reasonable.

CHAPTER II

An old man and an old woman sat together over a turf fire.

The old man had drawn his wooden stool so closely to the warmth that a thick pile of ashes had gathered round it; he spread his hands over the flame, and looked into it with vacant eyes and down-dropped jaw.

But the old woman had all her senses about her; her scanty grey hair was pulled back from her face and twisted into a tight knot at the back of her head; she was thin and bent, with sharp features and stern eyes. From the plates on the wooden dresser, which absolutely shone, to the earth floor, which showed in damp patches where it had been carefully levelled the day before, the cottage bore testimony to her active fingers. The old man could do nothing; once he had worked the loom which stood in the kitchen, filling it and leaving little but a passage; now he could not even be trusted to watch the bread and turn it at the right moments.

There was a batch of round soda-cakes baking over the fire now on a flat piece of iron which hung from the chimney by a long hook.

Mrs. Mawhinney watched them while she stitched at an old coat, and now and then paused to lift and turn them.

Windows and doors were hermetically closed—

the Mawhinneys had no undue partiality for fresh air, or even for sunshine.

The old woman looked up sharply when the half door swung open, bringing a rush of light into the cottage, and giving a glimpse of the lake, where it lay just below, glittering in the morning sun.

A very old woman stood in the doorway, a very dirty old woman, clothed in innumerable garments, which were all ragged, and which, in the course of unwashed years and endurance of all weathers, had faded to a uniform brownish tint. It was as if, on the wearing out of each article of attire, she had placed another on the top of it, till she had grown to be little but a mass of clothes.

It was not on record that Mary Ann Brennan had ever been known to take off a garment, even temporarily, much less to cast it away.

She was a very small old woman, and bent nearly double; there was little to be seen over the half door except a wrinkled, cheerful old face, with very bright twinkling eyes, surmounted by a succession of caps and bonnets, which had grown to a considerable height.

"The tap of the morning to you," said the old woman cheerfully.

Mrs. Mawhinney greeted her with sufficient cordiality. As a rule Mary Ann received a friendly welcome wherever she went; she brought with her the news of the county, and she was always cheerful, with a word for everybody.

"Come in and rest yourself; but pull to the door after you, for I want to keep the chickens off the floor till it's dried."

"And indeed and it's fine drying weather the day. I'll be glad enough of a rest, for I haven't set down since I left Wilson's up by the mill, and it's a long road for an old body, and wearyin' on the childer too."

Mary Ann found a stool for herself, and sat down with a breath of satisfaction, displaying a good deal of wrinkled bare leg, which the ragged ends of her petticoats failed to cover. Behind her half-a-dozen small dogs tumbled themselves into the cottage, and formed themselves into a decorous row by the fire.

Mary Ann distributed a few light taps and reproofs.

"Now, weans, you must be quite, and not be troublin' the good woman, if she lets you set by the fire. Whisht, Charlie, not a word out of you! How's himself the day, Mrs. Mawhinney?"

Mrs. Mawhinney had drawn her skirts well out of reach of the dogs. She did not like dogs, though, like everybody else, she tolerated those of Mary Ann.

"Well, he just doiters about—that's all he's fit for. The doctor has very bad behopes he'll put over the winter. I'll be sorry enough when it's the Lord's will to take him, but it's mortial inconvenient to be always looking after him."

The old man, crouched up in his corner, showed no sign of understanding; he was muttering and laughing to himself.

"Well, well! He's failed since I was in last," said Mary Ann, shaking her head sympathetically. "Quit, will you, Charlie; you're annoying the little ones."

Charlie was the least obedient of the dogs; he jumped against his mistress's knee, pulling aside her rags, from which came the whining of very young puppies.

"And it's the sough of the country that you're going to have a weddin' over in these parts."

Mrs. Mawhinney shook her head doubtfully.

"Ay, if Eccles Lindsay holds to the same mind. But I wouldn't trust him; he'll be taking up with some one else before the day. As for myself, I don't hold with marrying on foreigners; there's no being up to what outlandish ways they may bring with them."

"You'll not be thinking that when you see Nancy Jane. She's a fine swaddy, a real good wee worker, and not a lazy bone in her body. And then with a fortune. I think Eccles hasn't done that ill for himself. And it'll be a fine weddin'; there'll be two cars, and her sister to best maid."

"Be that as it may, it's in my mind that Eccles would have done better to suit himself with some decent wee girl hereabout, like his father before him. What call has he with foreigners from acrost the lake?" said Mrs. Mawhinney trenchantly. She proceeded to explain that she did not hold with travelling, and considered it an insult to the Lord to imply, as Eccles had done, that there was nobody good enough to marry without setting forth into unknown regions, eight or ten miles away.

Mary Ann Brennan listened, nodding her head, with remarks interpolated when it seemed necessary. "It's likely you're right." "I wouldn't say but that that's the way to look at it." "Well, well! it be to be like that."

The old man stretched his hands to a sudden bright jet of flame that came leaping from the turf, and laughed to himself. It was said that he had been a very stern man in his middle-age;

stiff in a bargain, stiffer even than his wife in what he considered his religious duties; but now the only thing that roused him to interest was a pipe or a cup of tea. On days when he could not get out and potter round he would ask for his tea incessantly, and cry if it was delayed.

There was something very cheerless about the three old people sitting there in the semi-darkness, with the light from two tiny windows almost blotted out by the huge loom.

Ellen Lindsay came in with a flash of youth and sunshine.

She was a pretty girl, with dark blue eyes and brown cheeks and fair hair, which gleamed when the sun shone on it. Ellen was almost a child still; she had not done growing, and she was half developed; but she was not awkward, and this was the most noticeable thing about her. There were plenty of pretty girls about Ballyturbet, but none who could move and hold themselves like Ellen.

She came in quietly, closing the door behind her in response to her grandmother's querulous commands, and with a nod to the old beggar-woman, knelt down and began to play with the dogs.

Her grandmother spoke to her sharply. Ellen was not a favourite of hers.

"What's come of you these last days, daughter? You haven't been down this length since Saturday."

"I'm very throng. My father's out till daily-goin', and it's all on me. I've the pigs' food to get, and that keeps me busy," said Ellen in her soft, pleasant voice.

"And I'll hold you you were at the lint-pulling

at Dawson's yesterday?" said Mary Ann; "and a terrible coorse evening they got for it."

"Ay, there's little fear of Ellen's being away when there was any dancin' or foolishness going. And I don't doubt your da was wakened up at all hours with you gettin' home. Well, it seems to be the way with the girls now to be always running; but when your mother was like you, I mind many's the month she wasn't across the door-step from week-end to week-end, barring to church and to the Sabbath-school. And now it's just dancing and worldly amusement you're thinking off, when a prayer-meeting would fit you better."

Ellen gave the faintest movement of impatience.

"I wasn't at Dawson's at all," she said. Somehow her grandmother's harsh, monotonous voice jarred on her this morning, but it was scarcely worth the trouble of justifying herself; Mrs. Mawhinney was certainly silenced, but only for a moment.

As for Mary Ann Brennan, she threw up her wrinkled hands in amazement.

"Well, well! how's that? I thought you were so great with Dawson's ones? But there's aye a good reason when a girl stays away from a bit of sport like thon; maybe there's somebody who wasn't to be there——"

Mrs. Mawhinney interrupted ruthlessly.

"There's foolishness enough in the wean's head without your putting more there, Mary Ann; so just hold your whisht. For one wasteful diversion she's stayed from there's many she's been to. If she was mine it's a different girl she'd be; no foolishness and nonsense then. Why, look at her now, running out of the house at this hour, and I'll be bound it isn't half tidied up. But there!

her father just spoils her, and she can come round him any road she likes."

"It's not easy to keep the place clean," said Ellen in a resolutely cheerful voice, "with the sow and the little ones in and out, do what you like; and there's no keeping the chickens off the flure unless the door is aye shut."

"And you can't expect the house to be minded if you're always running. If you were half as ready to spare the time for the Lord's service— but there! it was only the day I was speaking to Mr. Duffin about your missing church and Sabbath-school the twa-three Sundays, and I wasn't going to tell a lie, and says I, 'To the best of my belief, your reverence, it's nought but idle-set.'"

The colour flamed suddenly into Ellen's cheeks. She pushed back her stool from the fire, and got up abruptly, to the great discomfort of a couple of the little dogs which had established themselves comfortably on her knee. For a moment she thought of walking out of the cottage; then recalling with an effort her half-indifferent toleration for these accustomed reproofs, she went over to the corner of the dresser which was consecrated to her grandfather's pipe. Him, at least, she could easily make happy.

"My da sent you over a grain of tobacco, grandpa," she said.

The old man was eager and alert at once. Ellen made her way to him with some difficulty, as passage between her grandmother's seat and the loom was decidedly scanty; she knelt down beside him and began to fill his pipe, with the colour slowly dying out of her face.

Her grandmother, whose attention had been for the moment engrossed with taking the soda-scones off the fire and getting "a piece" ready for Mary Ann, woke up to what she was doing, and asked her sharply if she hadn't more sense than to give her grandfather his pipe when the tea was down to wet. The justice of the reproof was undoubted, and Ellen acknowledged it with her usual good-humour. She was very ready to be useful, and jumped up at once to fetch four substantial cups from the dresser; the old man, who had a tendency to lay his " piece ". on his knees butter side downwards, was also supplied with a plate, rejoicing in the picture of a little girl skipping in front of what was apparently a church tower in odd perspective; there was " A Present from Portnar " written underneath, and certainly, though in an artistic point of view the plate might leave something to be desired, it had been a constant source of satisfaction ever since Ellen had brought it back from a temperance excursion.

Mary Ann, after a tender inquiry for Ellen's puppy, which had been an offering from her, had floated off to talk of Eccles' marriage. As she talked she munched away contentedly at her piece of soda-bread, share and share about with the dogs, who were well accustomed to meals of bread soaked in tea. The mother of the three little puppies that travelled in Mary Ann's apron was engaged in her maternal duties, and had her luncheon laid aside for her, bit by bit. She watched her mistress with sharp black eyes which followed every morsel.

Mary Ann wanted to know all about Eccles' marriage—when it was to be; was he going to bring her home? was Ellen to have a new dress for the occasion? It gave her an opening for sundry jokes of the kind she found her audience generally appreciated.

"'One wedden brings another'—I don't doubt you've heard tell of that, Ellen? We'll be hearin' of you with a strapping boy of your own the next. It's just wonderful how a wedden sets folk thinkin'. Give me your cup, dear, till I look in the tay-leaves, and see if I can't promise you a handsome husband."

Mary Ann stretched out her hand, but Ellen drew away her cup with a hasty movement.

"It's all havers," she said.

"Not as much havers as you think, maybe. You wouldn't believe that I can see more than you fancy about the past and the future, and maybe name him you're thinking about now."

With a quick turn of her wrist Ellen flung the tea-leaves from her cup into the fire. She laughed uncertainly.

Mrs. Mawhinney had more or less dropped out of the conversation; she was very scornful of fortune-reading and "such-like foolishness," and she was kept busy enough drinking her own tea, and watching that the old man did not choke over his.

But just as Mary Ann was beginning to chuckle at Ellen's evident dread of her powers, the grandmother looked up with a sharp exclamation.

"Who's that going by the window? One of O'Neil's ones, I'll be bound. Heth! it's a quare thing a body can't have the way between their door and their midden to themselves! But it's like them Catholics—they're that crookit and onraisonable. But, come by our door to the well they shall not——"

"Sure, Mrs. Mawhinney, it's the minister," said Mary Ann.

Mrs. Mawhinney was on her feet in a moment.

"Sure, then, he'll be coming in. Ellen, take the tea-things ben, and bring a chair from the room. Where was it I laid that clean apron? Sit up, you ould gomerkal"—to her husband—"and give over licking your fingers. Ellen"—in an undertone—"give Mary Ann a lock of meal; she'll not go till she gets it. There's his reverence knocking—open the door till him, wean—what ails you?"

But Mrs. Mawhinney had to open the door herself; Ellen made no movement to obey her—gave no sign, indeed, that she heard.

The grandmother was one of the few left of the older generation who had been brought up to greet the "quality" with a curtsey. She dropped her curtsey now, and held out a hand of warm welcome, resolutely ignoring Mary Ann's attempts at greeting, which in the presence of her superiors she considered impertinent.

"Your reverence is kindly welcome. Will you come forrard to the fire and lain down. Ellen, did you hear me telling you to bring his reverence a chair from the room? You ould fool"—to her husband—"where are your manners? Rise up when you see his reverence. You'll excuse him, Mr. Duffin; he's a poor foolish old body, and doesn't rightly understand."

The old man laughed so heartily at this description of himself that he had to be picked out of the fire and rearranged on his stool before conversation could proceed.

Mr. Duffin seated himself awkwardly, with a few half-muttered words. He was a short, broad-set young man, with a coarse, good-looking face, and black hair and a black moustache, which was long and unkempt, and stood away from his lips. When he spoke he showed a row of small cruel teeth; his nose was a good one, but was indented with pimples, and his narrow, deep-set eyes were rather too close together. He wore his hair long, and plastered with oil, and was obviously none too careful about the brushing of his coat and the changing of his linen.

With it all the man was, in his way, handsome, and in the eyes of his parishioners, who admired black hair and red cheeks, he was "beautiful." That he was not a gentleman they knew perfectly well, and he had an uncomfortable suspicion that they knew it. But he was a clergyman, and as such deserving of all respect and attention.

He had come into the cottage with a suggestion of hurry in his manner, and a want of ease which was habitual in him; after one quick, almost furtive glance round, he sat with his eyes cast down, his head a little bent forward, and his broad, coarse hands, with their dirty nails, resting on his knees.

Old Mary Ann had had her portion of meal poured into her sack, and understood it as a signal to go. She collected her little puppies, shaking them back into their travelling-bag, from which their bright eyes gleamed out among her rags, and summoned the troublesome Charlie, who had gone off round the kitchen on an expedition of his own.

"May Heaven's blessings light on your reverence," she began as she moved towards the door. "It's a sight for sore eyes to see you, and you getting so stout—isn't that so, Mrs. Mawhinney?

I'm thinking your reverence wouldn't have the price of a grain of tea about you?"

"Now, Mary Ann, you mustn't be troubling his reverence."

"Well, I'll be giving him a call one of these days," Mary Ann assented cheerfully. "Long life to your reverence, and may you soon bring home a mistress. Come, childer, we must be getting on. I suppose your reverence wouldn't like to hear the childer cheer for King William— God bless him!—or give you their opeenion of the Pope?"

"That'll do, Mary Ann," said the unyielding Mrs. Mawhinney.

"Well, it'll be for another day. Good evening to you, Mrs. Mawhinney, and thank you kindly. May the blessings——"

Mary Ann got herself out of the house to a dropping fire of blessings, and tottered away down the road, with her "childer" keeping close to her bare legs.

Mrs. Mawhinney entered into voluble explanation. There was a complaining whine in her voice, which had come there through long years of taking the worst view of everything, and which was too habitual to be got rid of even on the rare occasions when she was *not* complaining.

"That's a foolish, godless old body, Mr. Duffin; it's a terrible thing to think how it will be with her when the Lord takes her. She has no more sense than to treat them dogs like Christians, and many's the time you might see her talking away to them, and singing light songs to them. And never a word of her latter end, which would be more fitting an old woman like her. Times and again I tell our Ellen it should be a warning to her—she's overly fond of treats and pleasurings. Ellen, rise up, daughter, and come and speak to his reverence—why, where's the wean gone?"

Ellen was not in the cottage; her grandmother had not seen her go, and marvelled how she could have slipped away so quietly. Mr. Duffin did not think it necessary to state that he had been more observant.

Mrs. Mawhinney apologised profusely for her granddaughter's want of manners.

"You will excuse her, your reverence? she's that backward and petted, and maybe she thinks shame you should see her with her bare feet. Her father can't make enough of her; you see, she favours the mother, and he's brought her up from a baby. The mother died when she was born. And Eccles and Willy are wild boys; Eccles is always after some petticoat or other, and Wully's very crabbit when the drink's in him."

The old man had finished his pipe, and after a futile attempt to fall into the fire, had taken up his tea-cup, and was amusing himself by licking up the few drops that remained with a smacking noise of satisfaction. His wife interrupted herself to take away the cup and reprove him sharply.

"Have done now! Quit, will you? and his reverence talking to me. You'll excuse his making so free? I was telling you about Ellen. Her head is full of foolishness, and I blame it on the reading; she still has her head in some silly story-book, but she won't be said by me. When I was like her it was very different. If we wanted to read, the one book was good enough for us; we just took down the Bible and read what was necessary for us."

Mr. Duffin, finding she paused, gave the expected murmur of approbation; Mrs. Mawhinney's opinions on any subject were supremely indifferent to him.

"And for me, I may say from the time I could read, there's not a day in my life I've missed my chapter, the Lord be thanked. There's not one chapter in the good book that I have not read over times and again to my pleasure and profit. And it was the same with our wee Annie—you'll mind I showed you the picture she sent us of herself out of America?"

Mrs. Mawhinney's remarks had wandered to a subject in which her guest took not the smallest interest; he had seen so many photographs "out of America" of girls with lace frills round their necks and silver lockets. He meditated an excuse for departure.

"Annie, now, would sit with her grandfather and me till I had to bid her go out, and there was hardly a hymn in the hymn-book she didn't know, and she could read us a chapter so beautiful! As for church—if you'd took and broken Annie's two legs she'd have got to church somehow! She was that petted on me—and a beautiful scholar—I'd just like to show your reverence a wheen of her copies I have up the room——"

Mr. Duffin rose precipitately. He had had more than enough of Mrs. Mawhinney, and he had not walked out to the lake, after long indecision, to talk to her. He disliked old women exceedingly, and they were in undue proportion among his parishioners.

"Some other evening," he said blandly, "I'll be calling in again passing——"

Mrs. Mawhinney said he was in a great hurry;

she would have considered it due to politeness to say this however long his visit had been. She escorted him to the door, still talking volubly.

"It's been overly kind of your reverence calling in again so soon, and you are most kindly welcome. It's lonesome enough down here, and I am not one that cares to kaly with everybody. And what's that poor old man but a care and a trouble? Then, you see, there's none of our own sort round here. Not but what for the most part they're agreeable enough, but you can't trust a Catholic; you never know when they'll turn on you. There's many a story I could tell you—but I see your reverence is pressed for time."

Mr. Duffin fiddled impatiently with his stick; he could not get his hand away from the old woman, who held it and patted it approvingly.

"It often comes as a trouble to me to think how it would have been if the battle of the Boyne had gone otherwise than as the Lord allowed it should," said Mrs. Mawhinney meditatively, "for true it is He does sometimes allow the devil's ones their way for the punishment of His people's sins. And it intrigues me to think——"

A sudden rush of chickens, encouraged by the open door, interrupted Mrs. Mawhinney's speculations, and gave Mr. Duffin a chance of escape of which he was not slow to avail himself.

He took his departure with more haste than ceremony.

CHAPTER III

The Reverend Samuel Duffin walked straight on down the lane till he was out of sight of Mrs. Mawhinney as she stood by her door, and had reached the road by which he had come. Then he paused.

He stood in the middle of a wide-stretching bog, with a narrow strip of road running through it, broken down and deeply rutted by the wheels of hundreds of turf-carts. Yesterday's rain had turned the cart-tracks into puddles, and even streams of water, between banks of velvety grey mud.

The wet bog had gained a brighter brown, with thick purple patches of heather and white cotton-grass, still a little dishevelled and dirty, to mark the soft places. Here and there were dark, still pools of bog-water outlined by tall rushes. Near where Mr. Duffin stood a drunken man had met his death only a few weeks ago; he had been found one morning with his face in the water, and his legs deeply embedded in the soft brown turf —quite dead.

Where the bog had been entirely cut away there were yellow fields of corn, and others green with flax. Over to the right a lint-pulling was going on. It was dinner-time, and the workers had gathered in a group at one end of the field;

two of the women had bright red petticoats, and white handkerchiefs tied over their heads to keep off the sun. Their talk and laughter floated over to Mr. Duffin where he stood, through the still air.

The smoke rose up almost straight from the cottage chimneys. The Lindsays' cottage lay the nearest, and was all by itself, with bog on every side. The lake was almost out of sight; just a gleam of it showed behind the poplars. There was sunshine on everything, making every bit of colouring vivid and definite. Mr. Duffin could even distinguish the green moss on the Lindsays'. thatched roof; in a corner near the chimney a growth of half-ripened corn shone like gold.

He hesitated, looking over the bog, himself an incongruous little patch of black in the middle of it.

He saw Ellen Lindsay come out at the house-door and gather an apronful of turf from a stack in the yard. She stopped on her way to drive back a brood of half-grown chickens that clustered round her, suspecting food.

Mr. Duffin's eyes followed her. She was certain to be alone; her father worked every day for a farmer called M'Cance, and Eccles and Willy were both hired out, and did not sleep at home. She had looked very pretty half-an-hour ago, with flushed cheeks and a strange look in her blue eyes which had made him vaguely uncomfortable.

He took a few uncertain steps in the direction of the cottage; as he did so he caught sight of a waggonette which was coming towards him at a quick trot, and he turned and came to a full stop, with a sudden change of ideas.

The waggonette was followed by a dog-cart and a pony-carriage, and all were full of people—a very festive party. It was a way the Barings and the Lawsons had of improving the last summer days. Having practically only each other to depend on for society, they often united and went for picnics and excursions. It was the dream and the ambition of Mr. Duffin's existence to be included in one of these expeditions.

He took a few steps in the direction of the carriage, frowning meditatively and pulling at his coarse moustache. If they saw him there—in their way, as it were—and if he made it evident by his manner that his time was by no means filled, would it not be likely that Mrs. Baring at least would ask him to join them? He went slowly towards them, subduing his pace to a saunter, swinging his stick, and cutting at the thistles and tufts of heather by the roadside.

Nelly Baring, who was sitting in the front of the waggonette, caught sight of him first, with an exclamation—

"There's that awful man! I shouldn't wonder at all if he tried to insist on joining us; he's quite forward and thick-skinned enough for that."

At that moment, had she only known it, Mr. Duffin was meditating a light, half-joking proffer of his society.

"Perhaps we ought to have asked him," Mrs. Baring said. "He certainly is very objectionable, but it's a lonely life——"

"It would have just spoiled it," said her daughter. "For my part, I don't see why the mere fact of a man's having 'reverend' before his name—a man you would otherwise send to the kitchen——"

There was a general "Hush." Nelly's voice was very loud and had well-known carrying properties, and they were quite close to Mr. Duffin.

He had almost made up his mind to say something—something that must be very light and casual—but at the last moment the words remained unsaid. Perhaps his courage failed him; perhaps the time was too short, and Nelly's curt nod too discouraging.

However that might be, a moment later he found himself standing alone on the road, a little splashed by the mud from the passing carriages. Their laughter and words faded slowly, and mingled with the voices of the lint-pullers.

Between them Mr. Duffin stood, a solitary figure. If Nelly Baring had seen the look on his face as they passed out of sight, she might have doubted his being so thick-skinned.

Samuel Duffin was the son of a farmer in the South of Ireland, who had succeeded in making farming pay. Samuel had been sent to a moderately good school, where most of the boys were above him in station, and where he had learnt a smattering of many things, and to despise his family. He had also become imbued with an ambition—which in such circumstances is not, perhaps, uncommon—to become "a gentleman."

An adoring father and mother had taught him diligently to think only of himself, and to think nothing beyond his power. At the same time he was no fool, and he understood that there were difficulties.

He set about making himself "a gentleman" methodically and doggedly, sacrificing much with a resolution worthy of a better cause. It was a small and petty ambition—a poor thing to make the desire of a life, as this young man understood the word. Still, it was the one thing which, being as he was, was utterly beyond his reach in every sense. Samuel Duffin would never be either outwardly or inwardly as a gentleman.

But, not unnaturally, he did not realise this.

The desire grew up steadily year by year in his mind, and became a resolution; he considered the matter carefully and to a great extent dispassionately—perhaps as dispassionately as it was possible for any one to consider a thing so personal. No man is prone to recognise that he is irredeemably coarser, more narrow-minded, less capable, than his fellows. Samuel Duffin saw clearly enough the defects in his speech and manner, and the disadvantages of his connections and surroundings, but thousands had overcome worse difficulties than these.

His father and mother were well-to-do for their class, but that was all. He realised—certainly unwillingly—that it was necessary for him practically to separate himself from them, and from their friends.

He persuaded his father without much difficulty to send him to Dublin, where he passed with credit through the divinity school in Trinity College; he worked so well, in fact, and brought with him such a good record as to character and diligence, that he found no difficulty in obtaining a curacy. It was a first step, and turned out to be much less of an advance than Mr. Duffin had hoped. His two years as a curate had proved eminently satisfactory to his rector, but very unsatisfactory to himself; he had not found himself sought after by the people he wished to seek him.

But he was by no means beaten or turned aside

from his object; he had given up too much, sacrificed too much, for that.

One of his fellow-students had laughingly accused him of living the life of an old woman. What it cost this coarse-blooded, passionate young Southern peasant so to live only he himself knew —the struggles with his temperament at every step, the many pleasant sins which tempted him almost beyond endurance.

But there was no medium for him, and he knew it; the stern life to which he condemned himself was his only safeguard. Without friends or interest, a character to which the most censorious could take no objection was his only way towards the object which had become almost a monomania.

At the same time, as far as his light went, Samuel Duffin did his duty as a clergyman; he worked hard and neglected nothing. Where the line was drawn between an honest desire to do what lay before him and a selfish regard for his own interest he himself honestly did not know.

He had not much advanced himself as yet. The better things he had hoped for on being appointed to Ballyturbet living a year ago had not yet come. Certainly it was a lonely place, and as rector of the parish he held a position which could not be ignored; Mr. Baring and Sir William Lawson, who were parochial nominators, and had had most to say to his election, had called, and in the summer Mr. Duffin had been once or twice invited to tennis parties, but the acquaintance had not grown more intimate.

Mr. Duffin had done his best; in the seclusion of the rectory he had rehearsed easy speeches and dignified but pleasing manners. But when the time came he found it impossible to look or seem at ease. The Lawsons and the Barings did not think about him at all unless he forced himself upon them, when they found the attempted familiarity of some of his moods even more intolerable than his occasional relapses into agonising embarrassment.

He might have had a cheerful life enough if he had been content to associate with the farmers round, but this he would not do. He was not going to relinquish his object so lightly; there was a dogged obstinacy about the man which would not let him confess defeat even to himself.

It was quite within his power to have been popular in the parish had he set the right way about it. He was in many ways fitted to please a Northern congregation. He believed devoutly in hell and the devil, and preached about them, and he hated Roman Catholics and Presbyterians with great heartiness. He was also absolutely clear from any ritualistic tendencies, and had no desire to progress in any way. To counterbalance these advantages, he was not a gentleman, and the peasants in the North of Ireland dearly love a gentleman; they were also quick enough to see that he gave them only half his mind and had no real liking for them; he talked to them always as a clergyman and never as a man, and was haunted by a fear of letting down his dignity.

So it came about that he lived apart from all classes, and the life was a terribly lonely one.

In a dim way some of these things passed through his head as the carriages rolled out of sight and he turned to walk towards home.

Such a dreary home as it was for one lonely man! The house was a fair one, but it looked dreary and depressing, with its four square walls and ill-kept avenue and steps. The church and meeting-house were almost opposite, and vied with each other in hideousness, and from the top windows of the rectory there was a glimpse of the chapel graveyard. Methodists, Plymouth Brethren, and a kind of mixture of the two called "dippers," carried on their séances at the other end of the one straggling street, which also boasted of eight public-houses. There was no lack of opportunity for quenching both spiritual and temporal thirst in Ballyturbet.

Mr. and Mrs. M'Cune lived at the Manse. As politics now were, Mr. M'Cune and Mr. Duffin were constrained to meet frequently at the Unionist Club, and at Orange and other political meetings. They were ceremoniously polite to each other, and united in condemnation of Roman Catholics, but in their secret hearts they hated each other worse still.

A dozen years earlier the sharp class distinction between Church and Presbyterian clergy had made everything simple; now the jealousy was of the bitterest, and cropped up in little things every day.

As Mr. Duffin turned up what he called the "avenue," and what an Englishman would have called the "drive," to his house, he exchanged a ceremonious bow with Mr. M'Cune, who was coming out of the Manse.

They met unavoidably almost every day, and jealously noted all each other's doings.

Mr. Duffin opened his hall-door with his latch-key and went in noisily, tramping down the little passage that did duty as a hall.

It was a most uninteresting little passage, with

a door to the right and left, and in front the stairs and another door which led to the kitchen. There were no possibilities for adornment, even had Mr. Duffin been a man capable of adornment.

An old woman's head was poked out of the dining-room to greet him—a dishevelled head of untidy hair over a queer, red old face.

She gave him a wavering smile, showing the absence of teeth so common in Irishwomen of her class.

"I have just been putting out the dinner for your reverence," she began effusively.

He cut her short impatiently; he was exceedingly tired of old women, and this old woman was to him particularly tiresome, because from her he could not escape.

"I see you've been at the whisky again, Betty. I tell you I'll get a decent lock put on the sideboard——"

The old woman waved a deprecating hand.

"Well now, I'll insense you into the reason of that, dear," she said, with unruffled amiability; "it's this terrible stuffing I have had ever since the brown katies last winter. When I have a wake turn I know it's not you would grudge me a taste of the only thing to relieve it."

Mr. Duffin pushed roughly past her.

"You'll have to go, that's all," he said. He had said it so often that the meaning had gone out of the words.

Betty Pollock was a legacy left him by the last rector, or at least she so considered herself, and a very troublesome legacy she had proved. Mr. Duffin had made several attempts to get rid of her, but in vain. She had been there all her life, and her mother before her, and she considered the rectory a great deal more hers than his. Rectors might come and rectors might go, but she went on for ever. As she told Mr. Duffin once, the rectory had never been without the blood of the Pollocks, and as long as she lived never should be. He had in some sort given in; and had tried to get girls under her to secure a certainty of having his bed made and getting something to eat with a fair amount of regularity; but this had not proved a success; Betty was bitterly jealous of the girls, and would not allow them to do anything, and it always ended in their departure in floods of tears.

He had become more or less used to Betty, but it was very dreary.

Mr. Duffin was a man who liked good food and comfort and cheerful faces.

The fire had gone out in the dining-room, and Betty had made an erratic attempt to lay the table. He knelt down on the hearth-rug and tried to light the turf with benumbed fingers. Betty staggered after him, and wept when she was not allowed to help. When a blue flame sprang up at last, he went to fetch his cold mutton and forage for potatoes for himself, and found her asleep in his chair when he came back.

That such a man endured it without turning her out of the house was a proof that Betty was the one person in the world he was afraid of.

CHAPTER IV

"Would your reverence be wanting any chickens? Wee Matty Bruce is at the door with a basketful."

"No, I don't want any."

"But there are but two pair left in the yard, and I'll hould you these are good ones——"

"I don't want any."

"But you mightn't get a chanst of such fine ones again——"

"I don't care if I never *see* a chicken again; I won't have them."

Mr. Duffin was sitting over the dining-room fire with a pipe in his mouth; he kept his back turned upon Betty, and drummed impatiently on his knee with a broad flat hand which was not so clean as it might have been.

It was a dreary day, a day on which Betty, and the fact that he could not be secure of the room to himself for five consecutive minutes, seemed particularly unbearable. A drizzling rain was falling every now and then, enough to make the prospect of an objectless walk untempting, and Mr. Duffin had been dragging out the afternoon dismally enough.

The room had a stale smell of ale and mutton; Betty had made several only half-successful attempts to take away the dinner-things. She had left the cover of the potato-dish and Mr. Duffin's plate on the sideboard, and had made no attempt to remove a cloth which was none too clean. What was the use, she would have said, when she would only have to put it back again for tea?

Perhaps with a similar idea, she had not troubled to dust the room for the last few days; when Mr. Duffin put up his hand on the mantelpiece to look for matches, he brought it back coated.

"Matty says that sooner than take them on, she'll give you the chickens for shillin's apiece——"

The reappearance of Betty's smiling, dishevelled head was too much for him. He walked to the door, pushed her out, and slammed it hopelessly, for he had long ago learned that a struggle with Betty was hopeless.

When he was alone his thoughts were not too pleasant. He had spent a year in this place—in this hole—and how had he advanced himself? That morning he had come upon a selection of Lawsons and Barings in eager conclave near the Barings' gate, and he had not failed to see the change — the sudden stiffening in the group as he came up. What they said and thought mattered to him only because they were a means towards an end, but in this way it mattered very much.

It was impossible for a man to exist in the society of old Betty alone.

Mr. Duffin was not imaginative, but as he sat looking into the fire a face seemed to grow out of the coals—the face of a girl with dark blue eyes and fair hair and a ready smile—a face which flushed and brightened when he was near. There was one person at least to whom he was the most wonderful, awe-inspiring, gracious person in the world.

But——

"Ould Mrs. Rooney's at the door."

He had not noticed Betty come in; now she had propped herself comfortably against the sideboard, and was smiling upon him benevolently.

"Ould Mrs. Rooney wants to see your reverence."

"What for?"

"She'll be wanting help. She says she's had a sore brash or she'd have been here sooner; and she says she'll never be back again, for she'll not see many more weeks."

Mr. Duffin tossed Betty a penny impatiently, with an intimation that he wished to see no more of her; but she was back with him in about two minutes, still smiling and amiable.

"She wouldn't take the penny at all, your reverence. She says she is down in the books, and she never got less than a sixpence. And indeed it's not much——"

Mr. Duffin got up and turned on Betty with an expression in his eyes which was by no means pleasant.

"And she'll be going to the Manse, and I wouldn't like them to say——"

"She may go where she likes—and you too. Didn't I tell you I wouldn't have you in here in this condition? You ought to be ashamed of yourself!"

Betty waved her hands in reproachful denial, an action which was fraught with danger to her balance; she turned deprecating, watery eyes upon her master, and showed her wrinkled, empty gums in a smile which was not a pretty one.

"Is it me? The Lord forgive you, dear! Me, that have never rested since your dinner except to sit down for a minit and read my Bible! Me, that can't thole the taste of whisky—not even when I had the brown katies and the doctor ordered it to me. If it wasn't for the wake turns and the toothache, never a drop would pass my lips——"

"Get out of this, you drunken old beast!"

Betty began to weep profusely, with many sniffs and sobs, applying her apron impartially to eyes and nose. It may be she had found tears useful to soften her former master, but on a man like Mr. Duffin they were wasted.

"And sooner than have them say ill words I would give a sixpence myself for the honour of the house; and me been here these forty years and never a complaint! But it's well said, the way of the righteous is thorny. Now I'm an old woman, I'll have to make place for some impitent cutty! But you'll be sorry for it; for all you miscall me you'll be sorry for it, and you'll miss me sorely. The Lord will provide; even if I am cast forth in my old age, I can trust in Him——"

Mr. Duffin turned upon her with a set underjaw and an angry flush in his coarse face.

"Hold your tongue!" he said. "If you are not out of this in extra quick time you'll be sorry for it—ye ould divil!"

There was nobody but old Betty to notice how strongly the Southern accent came out in his words, and she was a great deal too full of her own concerns. She was sufficiently herself to realise that her master looked dangerous, and she lost no time in getting herself out of the room, staggering and muttering to herself.

Mr. Duffin relapsed into a gloomy contemplation of the fire.

It was an unbearable life; it was *wicked* to condemn a man to it.

But he would not be beaten; all these years should not be wasted, and some day he would make his own place in the world.

Was he to let *one* mistake, *one* temptation, yielded to after so many had been resisted—was he to let this ruin him? A thousand times no! Let the fault rest with those who had condemned him to this life of isolation. But what a fool he had been—what a fool!—to run any risks.

The opening of the door did not even make him turn round. He only said roughly, "Get away, Betty! How often have I to tell you not to come in?"

"But there's a man——" Betty began in her cracked voice.

"I don't care who is there; I won't see any one at this hour."

"It's well for you I know better than to take you at your word, dear. I've no fancy to let your reverence sit and glower at the fire for want of company, and Dr. Morton wanting to see you, and he such a quare, good gentleman."

Mr. Duffin got hastily to his feet. Dr. Morton was rector of a neighbouring parish, a man in whose eyes he particularly wished to seem well, who was on intimate terms with the Lawsons and the Barings, and well thought of by all who knew him.

"Show him in at once," Mr. Duffin said.

He looked round the room uncomfortably, conscious that all was not as it ought to be, without knowing how to set it right. Had he known it, Dr. Morton was the last person to remark any deficiencies, or to heed them if he had.

He came in like a breath of fresh air, a tall, broad-shouldered man, with a cheery voice and the pleasantest manner in the world. It is to be supposed that Dr. Morton had troubles like the rest of the world; but if so, they sat upon him lightly, and by instinct it was the brightest side of everything and everybody that he saw. His laugh was most infectious.

He came into the room shaking raindrops from his coat, and Mr. Duffin went forward to greet him, nervously anxious to seem completely at his ease. He thought of addressing his visitor as "Morton," but was unequal to the effort. Certainly Dr. Morton was a very much older man, but as rectors their position was an equal one, he told himself, but he found it impossible to act on this assumption.

"It's a shame to come in upon you in this wet condition, Duffin. It's a disagreeable drizzle, and I am afraid it will interfere with the flax-pulling. I have got mine all in, I am glad to say."

"This is a great pleasure," Dr. Morton.

Mr. Duffin's manner of speaking was very deliberate, with hesitations and words carefully chosen and pronounced. He gave the impression, which was possibly a true one, of considering every word before he said it, to see if it was safe and suitable.

Betty was more hearty and less guarded. She insisted on being allowed to shake Dr. Morton's hand warmly, and burst into voluble speech.

"It warms my heart to see your reverence! I've been thinking you'd forgotten us altogether.

And how's the mistress?—and Miss Katie and Master James?"

"All flourishing, thank you, Betty."

"It's aye a heartsome thing to have a lock of weans about a house. I can't but say I find it lonesome here with no stir about. Your reverence should come over oftener, for sure I am you're more than welcome. I'm still telling the master he should visit more. When Mr. Dawson was wi' me, he was for ever going down to the Castle to play games of tennis and such-like, or they were up here, and it kept a stir. But now there's never one coming or going."

"That is sufficient, Betty. You may go," said Mr. Duffin hopelessly.

"There's no rank of life," said Betty, leaning against the sideboard and waving her hands, "but needs divarsions at times. The like of me—the commonality, as one might say—has their trips and their treats, and the quality has their own ways of amusing themselves. It's yourself that likes a bit of sport as well as any one, for all your black coat, Dr. Morton!"

"Oh, you and I are one in objecting to all work and no play."

"'Deed your reverence and I for ever think alike. I'm that uplifted to see you again, dear——"

Betty was seized with a further affectionate impulse; she staggered forward with outstretched hand.

Mr. Duffin came to the rescue in despair.

"Look here, Betty. Dr. Morton and I want to talk, and you must leave us in peace. You see what a disagreeable day it is, and how it is raining. Well, if you won't go away, Dr. Morton and I will have to go out, and you surely don't want to drive us to that?"

It may be that this pathetic appeal touched Betty; at any rate, a little later Mr. Duffin did contrive to get the door shut with her on the wrong side of it. He felt bitterly foolish and ashamed.

Dr. Morton turned to him with his hearty laugh.

"Your Caleb Balderstone is rather troublesome, I am afraid," he said.

Mr. Duffin had not the remotest idea who Caleb Balderstone might be. He said, "Yes, certainly," and smiled uneasily.

"I suppose you do find it a bit lonely?"

"Well, the parish is a small one; my time isn't half filled."

"And run over with old women, isn't it? I know Dawson used to complain that they never died."

Mr. Duffin smiled responsively; his idea of extreme politeness was to smile frequently.

"The people are all so poor," he said, "especially now that the weaving has practically stopped. All the richer farmers and shopkeepers are Presbyterians. There's a fair Sunday-school attendance in the morning, but Mrs. M'Cune works a good deal among the girls, and some of our girls will go to her in the afternoon. I think I shall be obliged to start an afternoon Sunday-school, and I am afraid the attendance will be very poor."

"I dare say Mrs. M'Cune won't hurt them. We Northerns are pretty stiff in our convictions," said Dr. Morton, with a laugh. "Well, I must get to business. I called to-day chiefly to ask if you are going up to the Protestant Orphan meeting next week, and also about the Sustentation Fund. The Archdeacon has asked me to suggest that at your next vestry meeting———"

Dr. Morton leaned back in his chair, with his elbow on the dirty table-cloth, and plunged into Church matters. It was difficult not to be at ease with him, he was so entirely at ease himself; and he grew so hot and eager over everything, that Mr. Duffin unconsciously found himself growing interested too. Dr. Morton got vehemently angry in discussing the encroachments of Presbyterians and the misdoings of troublesome vestrymen; but in the middle of his anger the comic side always struck him, and he laughed.

Towards the end, during a hot description of the woes of a rash curate, who had put up an altar-cloth with *I.H.S.* worked on it, and had found the letters cut off time after time—at the most exciting point of this tale Mr. Duffin's attention began to wander.

There were certain signs of departure about the other man; he had picked his stick from the floor and his hat from the table, and was sitting upright on his chair, instead of leaning back comfortably.

Ought he to be asked to stay for a meal of some kind? If so, what should the meal be, and how would Betty serve it? Was there anything presentable in the house in the way of eatables? Would it seem very inhospitable if he let his visitor start upon his eight miles' drive without any offer?

In the midst of his hesitation Dr. Morton got up to go, and Southern instincts got the better of doubts.

"Won't you stay to—tea?" Mr. Duffin said.

"No, thanks; I am going to drop in on the Barings and see if I can find somebody for a game of billiards."

How easily it was said! and yet surely the clergyman of the parish had as good a right to "drop in" on the Barings as any one else.

"I have half a mind to go with you," said Mr. Duffin, in a tone which he flattered himself was both natural and easy. At the same time he knew he was talking nonsense; that even under Dr. Morton's wing his courage was sure to fail at the last.

They had been sitting almost in the dark for the last half-hour, Mr. Duffin being unwilling to give Betty an excuse for returning by ringing for lights, and it was very dusky when they went out and walked down the street together.

Dr. Morton did not find his companion interesting, but he was given to take men as he found them; still, the other's obvious want of attention as they walked down the street made conversation difficult.

Mr. Duffin was hoping against hope that they would meet one of the Barings on their way, or, failing that, that he would have courage to follow his companion into the house as if it was the most natural thing in the world.

But neither of these things happened. As they came up the avenue he began to remember more and more keenly the many discouragements he had met with from the Barings, and he felt that before Dr. Morton they would be still more unbearable.

He answered on a sudden impulse when Dr. Morton asked if he was coming in—

"I don't think I will this evening; I have several things to do, and there's a Unionist Club meeting to-night."

Dr. Morton did not press him. "Well, then, good-bye, Duffin," he said. "Will you drive over to lunch one of these days? Mrs. Morton will be delighted to see you. And, you don't sing by any chance? We are trying to get up a concert for the schools, and musical talent is scarce."

Mr. Duffin said he did not sing, and they shook hands on the hall-door steps.

Inside, the lamps were all lighted, but the shutters had not yet been closed, and through an open window a hum of voices with breaks of laughter came to Mr. Duffin; he could hear the momentary pause, and then the welcoming greeting which followed Dr. Morton's entrance.

Above them all came Nelly's clear, loud voice: "We won't let Dr. Morton go till after dinner, will we, mamma?"

It occurred to Mr. Duffin that any one who saw him standing there in the dusk and the rain might think it odd, and he turned away abruptly. To be outside seemed his place always—out of all cheerfulness and companionship—solitary always.

It did not occur to him to wonder if it was in part his own fault.

"Curse it!" he said between his teeth.

CHAPTER V

It was a day to make any one feel inclined to be idle, a wonderful day for September, with soft, warm breezes, and sunshine which made the lake look like silver.

Ellen and the puppy had felt they could stay indoors no longer, and had come out to join the father and Eccles in the flax-field.

Now that the lint-pullings of larger people were over, the Lindsays had got a day off to attend to their own little bit of cut-out bog. It was only a strip where the turf had been all cut away sooner than in other places, but it was their very own, and they thought a great deal of it.

Ellen lay lazily among the flax, half watching the others, half inattentive, her water-cans and wooden hoop bearing witness that she had not come out entirely in idleness. The path to the well went right through the field—"along the cash, and through the slap and out by the shough," as Mrs. Mawhinney had once directed a bewildered Englishman.

Ellen had found herself a very comfortable corner; she lay with her arm across her eyes to keep off the sunshine, which fell warmly on her hair and her bare feet. It was only of late that she had begun to feel the loneliness of her life. To-day she had a sense of satisfaction in knowing that her father and brother were so near; it helped her not to think, and to lie there and enjoy the sunshine like an animal.

If she had seen her grandmother coming she would probably have beaten a hasty retreat, but her eyes were hidden by her arm, and if she moved it she only caught a dazzled glimpse of blue sky straight above her. Mrs. Mawhinney's harsh voice in her ear was the first announcement she got that her dreamy contentment was over.

As usual, Mrs. Mawhinney was anxious and troubled about many things. She began with a very favourite topic of hers—the ill-doings of the M'Faddens, who would persist in using a right-of-way they had past her cottage to the well. This was the injury which of all injuries seemed to Mrs. Mawhinney the most unbearable, and be the conversation what it might, she always managed to bring in a reference to it.

Lindsay and Eccles came up before she had half finished and changed the current of her thoughts.

Eccles was a tall, stout young man, with an unkempt appearance and no manners. He was kindly and good-natured enough, and much more popular in the neighbourhood than his brother " Black Wully," as he was called, partly owing to his dark hair, and partly to his terrible temper. " Black Wully " was a furious Orangeman and remarkably strong, and had got into trouble more than once or twice; he was an excellent Churchman as far as hating all other denominations went, though he seldom or never went to church. Eccles, on the contrary, was liked by everybody, and was quite content so long as he was able to take life fairly easily, and to get a bit of amusement now and again which cost nothing; for he was very careful of his money.

He was glad now to throw himself down on the flax beside Ellen, wiping his hot face and taking out his pipe.

Old Lindsay was in a cheerful frame of mind.

"We've a fine crop the year," he said; "I don't mind when it was as good. And if the potatoes turn out as well—and I've no reason to think they won't—we'll do rightly."

"Ay; but the better the crop the cheaper it is to sell," said Mrs. Mawhinney, shaking her head; "and them that knows tells me there'll be next to no weaving the year, and that'll come hard."

"There's still something turns up," said Lindsay, undismayed. "Did you hear we'd a letter from Philadelphy last night, and Mary and Andy sent two pounds to me and as much to Ellen? And they'll send something more by Christmas. And what with that and the crop I'm gey uplifted."

"You needn't count on help from them for long. It's all very well at the first, but wait till they've begun to forget and got married maybe. That'll be another story."

Lindsay gave a good-humoured laugh.

"Hark till her! I never put up a feather that she doesn't pluck it out of me! You're aye setting off in a coach-and-four to meet your troubles, grandma."

"I've small need to do that, then," said Mrs. Mawhinney dolefully; "they're not far to seek. If I saw my own following in the Lord's path, it's little I'd think of this world's troubles. But when I see them stubborn and onreasonable, neglectful of their duties to their God in attending the church and the Sabbath-school, not content with the home He has given them, and wanting to leave all behind them and go to service—— The Lord knows, Jamie, if you've been too easy with the authority He has put in your hands, I have done my best."

The words fell on silence. Ellen moved impatiently, and Eccles began to fill his pipe stolidly. Mrs. Mawhinney's harsh voice seemed to destroy the peace of the day; but for her it was so still that they could hear the soft splash of oars on the lake, and the cry of the "peewits" that flew over it. The whistle of a train three miles away sounded shrilly.

"What call has Ellen to go to service? I don't say that many as good or better than her don't go and no disgrace about it, but while her father can keep her at home she's better there. If her head wasn't full of foolishness she would never have thought of it. But there she goes, ready for any amusement, and in for an hour yesterday colloguing with those M'Faddens just as if they were her own sort. She'll be turning next."

Eccles gave a grunt of disapprobation. "You needn't even the like to Ellen," he said. "You might as well say Miss Nelly would be turning—many's the time she's in to M'Fadden's."

"It's very different for the quality from it is for the like of us," said Mrs. Mawhinney. She was fairly started on one of her subjects, and was in her glory. "Times and again I tell Ellen never to trust a Catholic, but it's little she minds what I say. They are deceitful to the heart's core. Wasn't it James Dougherty, a friend of my own—married on my father's sister—that took up greatly with a Catholic boy when he was a lad? They were always together and as great as could be. And you'd have thought James was clean out of his mind when the other boy took sick and was given over by the doctor. He was for setting up with him night and day. And the night the Catholic boy died, he called James to him, and says he, 'James, are we alone?' and James says, 'Yes.' Then says he, 'Bend down your head, James, till I whisper.' And says he, 'Never trust a Catholic.' And James was all surprised, and says he, 'Haven't we been great enough?' And the Catholic boy says, 'Ay, James, you've thought so; but many's the time, when we were out together, I had a knife under my coat ready to murder you.' And that's gospel truth, and you know it, Jamie Lindsay."

If he did not, it was not for want of hearing it, for the story was by no means new to him. Ellen breathed more freely now that the conversation had turned from her delinquencies.

But Mrs. Mawhinney had not nearly finished.

"And only the other day Burnside Overend was walking twelve miles to some fair looking for a cow, and he was overtook by a Catholic in his cart. And he offers him a lift, and Burnside was thankful enough to get it. And they hadn't gone very far, and were just down along the Lough shore, where they're all the wrong sort, when the Catholic began to shout, 'To hell with the Pope!' and 'No Home Rule!' and every Protestant cry he could think of. You see, he knew that, if any Catholics heard it, they'd come running out and take it to be Burnside that was calling, and him sitting quite. By luck nobody heard him, or Burnside would hardly have seen his home again, and you may be sure he was out of the cart pretty quick. But that's the sort they are, Jamie. There's a bad drop in them all."

Lindsay nodded his head assentingly. In the main he agreed with his mother-in-law, and was as bitter against the Catholics in a body as she could wish, though he was too good-natured to share her animosity to individuals.

"You'll never find a Catholic to be trusted," Mrs. Mawhinney reiterated; "if I had my will, never one of them should cross my step. I was just saying to the minister yesterday, 'Your reverence,' says I, 'if it's not making too free, I've been thinking a soft hat would be more becoming to you.' And says he, 'Why's that, Mrs. Mawhinney?' He's a pleasant-spoken gentleman enough. And says I, 'Sure it used to give me pleasure to see you walking down the road, but now in the distance I can hardly tell whether it's you or the priest.'"

"The minister and you seem very great. He's aye dropping in for a kaly with you," said Lindsay, laughing.

"He's a religious man and a good preacher—a very serious speaker, and preaches the true gospel. It would do Ellen a wheen of good if she would go to hear him constant. I bid him speak to her the very last time I saw him about her neglect of the school of a Sabbath and her wanting to go to service. And I hope you'll mind what he says to you, Ellen."

Ellen's head was bent over the puppy; she murmured something indistinct, and did not raise it.

"Ellen's well enough," her father said shortly.

"It's ill done of her to go again' the minister, and him so good to her at the first."

D

"I wouldn't like that. I hope the minister's not ill-pleased with you, daughter?"

There was a short pause, a pause just long enough to be perceptible.

"Don't trouble yourself about that," said Ellen in a rough voice.

"For he's been very good about Wully, and I'd like you to do your best to please him."

Ellen jumped suddenly to her feet with an abruptness of movement which was quite unusual to her.

"I'm just wearied with having you all at me!" she said passionately. "You'd think I was that ill-mannered that nobody could put up with me! I'm—I'm fit enough to mind myself!"

She turned from them sharply with a movement of uncontrollable nervous irritation, and hurried across the field with quick, uncertain steps, leaving astonishment behind her; Ellen, as they knew her, was so sweet-tempered, so little inclined to be touchy.

Eccles gazed after her with wide eyes.

"Keep us! what ails our Ellen?" he said.

"Heth! she's in a quare pucker," said her father. "I'm ignorant what has come over her these last weeks. She was finely set up at the first with the minister thinking well of her in the choir."

"And Ellen was aye one that liked to be taken notice to," the old grandmother said. "I mind well, when she was a wee wean, she came home from the school roarin' and cryin' fit to break her heart, and for long enough we couldn't get out of her what ailed her. At last says she, 'Sure, grandma, Mr. Wilson'—him that was the minister then—'he come into the school when we were readin', and he wrote something in Annie Cregg's copy-book, and he pulled Eva Jackson's ear, and he took no notice to me though I was right fornenst him.' And with that she to the roarin' and cryin'."

During this thrilling anecdote Eccles' attention had wandered; he had his own troubles to think of, and they drove Ellen out of his head as he sat and puffed at his pipe. Only her father's eyes followed her into the cottage.

Ellen went in hastily, slamming the door after her, and narrowly avoiding making an end of the puppy, which had found some difficulty in keeping up with her rapid movements.

But with this her energy seemed to go. She sat down on a stool by the fire, heedless of the puppy, which had had its foot pinched, and was very sorry for itself, and making a great fuss in consequence.

She sat with her hands clasped together till they hurt, and her soft lips set. For the first time in her life she was facing a trouble which seemed unbearable, and realising that it had come to *her* with the surprise and rebellion of all young creatures against their first pain. She knew there was suffering—plenty of it—in the world; but that it should come to *her!*

The puppy, in a small way, was going through the same experience.

CHAPTER VI

"Well, bring them as soon as they are fit to kill. You haven't done well with your chickens this year."

"The early ones throve rightly; you'll mind I brought Mrs. Baring some fine birds in the spring, Miss Nelly. But I don't know what come over these two last clatchings."

"Your ducks are better than ours, I see. We must get a setting from you next year. And now, Ellen, what has happened to you lately? You haven't been to Sunday-school or church for weeks, and you missed the last girls' friendly meeting."

Miss Baring stood in front of Ellen, a brisk, decided little figure, with short petticoats and thick boots, and a dog-whip and whistle, which were supposed to keep in order a couple of lawless setters, at present poking with eager curiosity through the Lindsays' yard. She took Ellen to task in a clear, rather hard voice.

Ellen had been filling her basket from the turf-stack; she leant against the brown background drawing lines in the mud with her bare feet; a dull red crept gradually into her round, childish face.

She said nothing till Nelly Baring repeated her question rather sharply.

"Now what has kept you away, Ellen?"

"The work's been very throng." The girl's answer came almost under her breath.

"Not on Sundays, surely? Ellen, it is good, steady girls like you that we want particularly to stick to Sunday-school and classes, not only for your own sake, but to influence others."

Ellen's head sank lower.

"You will soon be a woman," Miss Baring, who was four years older, began with much confidence.

Ellen, with her face turned away, listened to an essay upon womanhood according to the brisk little girl in front of her, who had only touched the outside of life, and so was able to express herself after the gloriously trenchant fashion of ignorance.

The cottage lay between them and the lane, and shut them out from passers-by; if it had not been for this, Mr. Duffin would certainly not have come upon them round the turf-stack with a suddenness which made them both start. Ellen confronted him with a look of positive terror in her blue eyes.

Miss Baring made a wonderful effort to be civil; instead of making her escape at once, she actually stayed, choosing subjects she considered suitable, and trying to draw the other two into harmony. The possibility that she might not be producing general gratification never entered her head.

"Maybe," Ellen broke in in a low voice, "I had as well go in and see that the cats are out of the road, for fear the dogs would hunt them."

She went without waiting for an answer. Miss Baring, a little surprised at her abruptness, turned graciously to Mr. Duffin.

"Nice girl, isn't she?"

He assented shortly.

"But such a baby still. I have seen her playing with that little red-headed M'Gloughlan as if they were both the same age, and certainly Ellen doesn't look sixteen. One would have thought having to keep house for her father would make her into a woman, but I am sure I don't know what will."

Mr. Duffin said nothing. Perhaps he did.

"Well, I suppose I mustn't keep you if you are parish visiting," said Nelly, still with much condescension. "I am going to see poor M'Fadden, but he belongs to Father Dymond. Good morning; wonderful weather for this time of year, isn't it?"

Miss Baring wondered why she had found him so much more speechless and less objectionable than usual; in truth, Mr. Duffin had not had time to collect himself or bring himself from the mood in which he had made his way to the Lindsays."

When Ellen had been called out to say good-bye, and Miss Baring had whistled to her setters and disappeared down the lane, a long pause fell between the other two.

Mr. Duffin played with his stick as if his chief object in life was to make it draw an exact circle in the mud; from time to time he gave rapid, half-stealthy glances at the girl.

"Ellen," he said softly.

Ellen drew her breath sharply.

"I'm skeared at your coming."

"Nonsense; it's safe enough—there's no fear."

"I've black fear at my heart. There's no call for you to come; it's a foolishness." There was a hurry in Ellen's soft voice; she looked round her nervously, and the colour came and went in her face.

Mr. Duffin went closer to her, and laid his hand roughly on her arm.

"Meet me this evening, then," he said, and she interrupted with a sharp cry of pain.

"No, no, no! Didn't you give me your solemn word——"

"I can't keep it."

The two stood looking into each other's faces in a moment of silence; then Ellen drew back, quivering and hiding her face from what she saw in his eyes.

"I don't care what I promised—you *must* come."

Ellen's words came in hurried, passionate appeal, with sudden pauses where her breath failed her.

"I couldn't do it, sir! For God's sake don't ask me—till I try to be a good girl—but I can't be—never, never again."

"Don't be a little fool," said Mr. Duffin hoarsely. "I tell you I can't stand much of this. Ellen——"

The girl recoiled in sharp terror.

"Don't come near me. I wish I was dead, God forgive me! For your own sake and mine, go away, sir. There'd be murder done if my father or the boys——"

"I'll go if you'll meet me this evening——"

"I can't, I can't, I *can't*—God help me!"

Ellen broke into bitter sobbing, but she would not yield; Mr. Duffin tried passionately, with rough words, to beat down her resistance. He was excited beyond his own control, and almost forgot his fear of observation—almost, but not entirely.

Ellen had always given in in the end; perhaps

she would have given in now had not a sudden remembrance that when Miss Baring left the M'Faddens' cottage she must see them made Mr. Duffin's patience break down suddenly. He let go his hold of her arm and pushed her from him roughly, with a coarse word of anger.

"You little devil, do you want to drive me mad?" he said. "You are setting up to be particular—a trifle late."

Ellen watched him, as he made his way hastily down the lane, with vague, almost indifferent, eyes. It was impossible that it was to her, Ellen Lindsay, that this thing had happened, that her life was spoilt just as she was coming to a full enjoyment of it.

She felt in a strange way outside herself, as if it was another person she pitied—another poor girl for whom she was so sorry, that sharp, painful tears sprang to her eyes; it could not be herself.

It was time to bring in the goats. Ellen, by force of habit, shut the house-door to keep out the chickens, and picked up a stick in case the grey goat should be troublesome.

She had a little way to walk across the bog to the green patch where they were tethered, and she surprised herself actually singing softly as she went, picking her way round bogholes and soft places.

Yet it was true—it was real—it had happened to her.

She had tried, tried so hard to forget, to put away all thought from her and just live in the present. She was so very young—she had remained such a child—that sometimes she had succeeded.

But Miss Nelly. Ellen had been very fond of

Miss Nelly, after whom she had been named, and whom she had known all her life. But never, never again would she go to Sunday class or to Miss Nelly's meetings.

Ellen was only just beginning to realise her misery that evening as she walked over the bog; at first the overmastering excitement which had been brought into her life had driven out other thoughts.

She had grown up so quietly and drably. She had never been free like other children, though her father had done his best for her; but she had had to "mind the house" almost before she could reach up to lift the pot off the fire.

And she had been very strictly brought up—to believe almost everything in the shape of amusement was wrong. The greatest excitements of her life—next always to "the twelfth"—had been occasional Methodist or Plymouth Brethren meetings, as a variation of the usual round of week-day work and Sunday-school and church.

Then this had come into her life, upsetting and bewildering all her ideas of right and wrong, and throwing her among problems neither her age nor her education fitted her to face.

Protestants who went regularly to church were good and were saved; others were bad, and certainly not among the elect. Clergymen were to be reverenced, and at the same time to be sharply watched lest they should fall into High Church errors, but in nowise to be regarded as on the plane with the rest of mankind.

This easy classification was upset.

Ellen was exceedingly capable of taking care of herself with young men of her own class; she held her head high and kept them at a distance.

But when the minister — the minister who preached to her in church and taught her in Sunday-school—who sometimes went to have his dinner at "the Castle," and talked to Miss Nelly on terms of equality—when he began to notice Ellen a little more than the rest, she was pleased and flattered.

Never for an instant did she think of herself and him as woman and man till he absolutely forced her to think. Then, in a whirl of vanity and bewilderment, it seemed to her now she had for the time lost her senses, and lived without thought, in a mad, hidden excitement.

She had been proud—yes, *proud*—of her conquest of this demi-god, who left Miss Nelly to come to her. To Ellen he was the handsomest, most fascinating, most irresistible person in the world, and she was a girl to feel the full influence of difference of rank.

Only lately the shame had broken upon her, and begun to crush her down; she had not been ashamed at first.

Necessarily in Ellen's class everything was understood. She had often heard the neighbours talk of girls—such as she was.

She knew exactly what they would say, and the tone in which they would say it—their contemptuous interest and pity, their untiring discussion of this choice bit of scandal.

Her grandmother—Ellen knew how bitter, how unforgetting her tongue could be; and her father? —she liked to think of him least of all—it would just break his heart.

She did not distinctly blame any one. In her class no question of equal morality for men and women had ever been raised. A girl who did not know how to take care of herself was a fool, and worse.

Men were—as God made them.

The white goat came the length of her tether to meet Ellen. She was surprised to find how long her mistress took to unfasten the rope, and came to poke her nose in curiously and see what the difficulty could be. Ellen got to her feet and walked slowly back, very slowly, though the white goat tugged at the tether to hasten her.

It was unbearable, unbearable. She was a wicked girl, and God punished the wicked; but she would be good—so very good—if she could have another chance—just one more chance; she had been such a child, and so foolish before. Was it just to let her spoil her whole life before she understood what she was doing? Was it just to leave her hopeless at sixteen? And all she wanted must be such a little thing to God—just one more chance.

From how many poor souls this prayer of Ellen's has gone as an exceeding bitter cry—the useless prayer for one more chance.

CHAPTER VII

The M'Faddens' cottage lay close to the bog road. Barclay M'Fadden's bed was drawn up to a window in the kitchen which looked out upon it, and from which he could see passers-by when there were any.

Sometimes a neighbour stopped his turf-cart in answer to the patient face by the window, and left his old horse to stand with hanging head and quivering legs while he went in to chat with Barclay. Often enough one of the Lindsays would drop over to smoke a pipe by the fire.

Ellen never forgot to give him a nod and smile as she passed, and whenever she gathered a bunch of golden gilgowans, or primroses, or sweet white violets, half at least went to stand in a blue jug by his bed.

It was four years ago now since Barclay had had his back injured by a fall of iron from a cart he was loading. He had only kept to his bed for a fortnight at the time, and had then gone back to his work, with intervals and irregularities, for nearly a year. Then gradually the days on which, with the best will in the world, he could drag himself out grew fewer, and at last ceased altogether, and he was reduced to spending his time in a chair by the fire.

A month or two later even this had become an

effort, and it was more than a year now since he had left his bed.

His sister was a dressmaker, and also kept a shop in the other kitchen window. Her stock was displayed on three shelves decorated with very elaborately cut and very dirty pink paper, and consisted of various wooden boxes, filled indiscriminately with sweets in an advanced stage of stickiness, gingerbread figures, salt herrings, and reels of thread. Miss M'Fadden described herself as being fond of having things pretty, and the kitchen walls were adorned with little brackets in coloured paper, artificial flowers out of old hats, coloured prints with shell or straw frames, and similar things of beauty. Unfortunately she was not equally fond of having things clean, and all her decorations were coated inch-deep in dust.

They lived on what she earned, with the addition of three shillings a week, which was allowed them by a well-to-do nephew. This nephew was the pride of the family, and never failed to enter into his aunt's conversation, and he had certainly done well. He had begun by keeping a successful public-house, and now represented his county very noisily and vehemently in Parliament. And he neither forgot nor neglected his family; in addition to his weekly allowance, he very often sent them presents.

There had been something of a fuss made over Barclay at the beginning of his illness; he had been active and hard-working, and everybody had a good word to say for him. He had plenty of visitors, and all were on the look-out for the chance of doing him a kindness.

The Lawsons and the Barings brought jellies

and soup, and linen for his back, and produced an occasional unasked half-crown.

That was three years ago.

But the illness had gone on so long—months and years had passed with so little change.

Even Nelly Baring was ashamed to find herself often forgetting him for weeks together, though she liked to walk over the bogs, and knew that the books she brought him were all the help he had to pass the days.

When she had said good-bye to Mr. Duffin she discovered that the setters had preceded her into the cottage; and as they were animals of restless disposition, with lax notions of honesty, the first thing to be done was to turn them out.

Miss M'Fadden said, "Sure, never you mind, Miss Nelly dear; if they do take a drop out of the hens' bucket there's no great harm."

But her protest was obviously made only for politeness' sake.

"You are looking bravely, Miss Nelly," said Barclay from the bed. "It's heartsome enough while this weather lasts."

"No rheumatism now, I hope?"

"Heth! he's just dwining away. You'd think he'd been blinked. He'll never see another lint-pulling."

Miss M'Fadden spoke as if she was making a joke; she was handicapped by nature with a fat, irremediably cheerful face. She was an exceedingly stout person, with a soul above toilet cares. Her hair was partly encased in plaits, partly hanging down her back, and partly standing up on end, but entirely unkempt. Her red bodice had been enlarged by insertions of a different cloth under the arms, and even with this assistance burst away from the buttons and pins which held it across her ample breast. Beneath it the brown skirt gaped open at the side with a vista of petticoats, ending abruptly half-way down a pair of stout legs encased in wrinkled black stockings.

When Miss M'Fadden got up to bring Nelly a chair she had an air of holding on her clothes during the effort.

"I was badly taken yesterday with pains under the oxter—saving your presence," said Barclay; "but it's aye up and down, and we must be content with what the Lord sends us. That last book was very interesting reading, Miss Nelly. They were right and quarrelsome in them days."

"Barclay was finely taken up with it," said Miss M'Fadden; "he read out a good wheen to Eccles Lindsay last evening."

"And talking of Eccles Lindsay, isn't he going to be married?" said Nelly Baring.

Miss M'Fadden's fat face broke into smiles.

"Heth! he may or he may not. The sough of the country says that he has three of them coorted up to the axing. Sure, he's so terrible hard to please, I believe I'll have to take him myself!"

Miss M'Fadden laughed at her own joke heartily, shaking all over and bursting an insecure button.

"Eccles is smart enough," she said, "but it's Ellen is the white-headed boy of that family. Barclay, there, can't think enough of her, an' I'm aye telling him that as soon as he's fit to rise he will be leaving the priest and going off to Mr. Duffin for a weddin'."

When his sister's laugh had subsided and he

could hear himself speak, Barclay supported Ellen's praise.

"She's a good, religious wee girl," he said, "and she might be fifty she couldn't mind her father better, and I couldn't tell you the times she's been in with a nosegay of flowers or an extry baked cake. There's not one she ever forgets. What did she do but come in yesterday with a frame for Sarah Jane's picture of the Queen that Johnny sent till us, and the straws all cut beautiful and tied with blue ribbon, too. She's a terrible thoughtful wee girl."

"Johnny" was the Home Rule member. Nelly Baring always welcomed the appearance of his name in the conversation, and held it there now by a prolonged inspection of the picture.

The Queen, with very red cheeks and a gold brooch, smiled placidly out of a surrounding of straw and ribbons, and Miss M'Fadden said she was "beautiful."

"No doubt Johnny has many opportunities for seeing her. I'm thinking of going up to London myself and bidding him get me to tea with her. I'd look fine among the quality."

Miss M'Fadden's laugh broke out again with hearty energy.

"You might go and speak for Home Rule," Nelly Baring suggested.

"'Deed and what would hinder me? There wouldn't be another word out of Lord Salisbury and the rest of them if a fine sonsy young lady the like of me got up to show them the rights of it."

"Hear till her!" Barclay commented, his sister being too much overcome with her own wit to proceed.

"Well," said Nelly, "when you get back to Ireland afterwards, I hope you will often come to the workhouse to see us."

"Heth now! maybe it won't do you so much harm as you think——"

"More harm than it will do you good, I fancy. Now, what do you expect Home Rule to do for you?"

Miss M'Fadden had got back to the blue serge skirt she was getting ready for machining. She looked up and laughed.

"I couldn't rightly tell you, Miss Nelly, but them that's wiser than me says it will do good."

"It will hardly leave us worse than it finds us," said Barclay.

"But how will it make you better?"

"Sure, they say every one will have their rights. And there's the gold-mines——"

"Oh, the gold-mines!" said Nelly. "Do you really think that if there were gold-mines worth working they would have been neglected all these years?"

"I'm not scholard enough to understand," Miss M'Fadden said, settling her work in the machine, "but them that's wiser than me——"

"Well, if that's all you can say in your speech, I am afraid you won't convince Lord Salisbury," said Nelly in her most trenchant tones.

But the M'Faddens only laughed with much good-humour.

CHAPTER VIII

"I NEVER do a good action that I don't sorely repent it."

"My dear Nelly, I can only say that I am horribly scandalised."

A selection of Barings and Lawsons was established under the trees in the Barings' garden, contentedly eating unripe cooking apples.

Nelly, always the leading spirit, had established herself on a low branch, and with her tennis-racquet for a table, was busily fashioning a procession of cows and pigs from particularly hard windfalls.

"It's true enough," she said, shaking her head; "Dr. Morton gave me a long lecture last time he was here about being nicer to Mr. Duffin, and trying to talk to him sometimes."

"I know. I heard him saying much the same to Katie and the mother," said a young Lawson, "about his lonely life and efforts to do his best, and that one ought to sow seeds of kindness."

"All very well if one did not reap a harvest of calls three hours long! As sure as I speak civilly to Mr. Duffin one day, he comes and spends the next afternoon here. There, Jack, you can have my racquet if you are going to play any more tennis. And see if you can get that last cow to stand up; I was making it when I heard that

Mr. Duffin was here, and cut its leg too short in my disgust."

"Why, there's no need for you to go in. Mrs. Baring is there, and Adela."

"Oh, it's my fault; I must take the consequences," said Nelly recklessly.

In truth, Miss Baring had no confidence in the capability of her family to receive an afternoon call or do anything else without her.

She ruled them very firmly, if kindly and for their good.

Mr. Duffin had indeed come full of the remembrance of her civility of the day before, of which he felt himself to have taken too little advantage. Was he beginning to break down the vague barrier, and would it do to accept Betty's often-repeated suggestion, and ask them over for tennis at the rectory?

He sat on the edge of his chair, and spoke in careful sentences, till his want of ease flashed upon him, when he went to the other extreme, lounging and being elaborately careless.

He made two attempts to get to the subject of his invitation.

Once he asked Nelly if she was "addicted to the game of lawn-tennis;" and, failing to make the most of this opportunity, he inquired from Adela later on where the best lawn-tennis bats were to be obtained.

But Nelly held the conversation, and turned it decidedly to parish matters; she considered it her duty to keep him up to the mark.

Had he been to see Lavinia Bruce, and had he spoken to Eccles Lindsay about taking the pledge? Did he know that when the Pattersons' cow died they actually believed it was "blinked," and gave "the wise man" a pound to come and cure it? Had he heard that poor old Mary Ann Brennan was to have her dogs taken away because she could not pay for licenses?

Then came long pauses, but by this time Mr. Duffin's courage had ebbed.

He *could* not find words now to give his invitation in terms of easy equality. It occurred to him that it might be best after all to write, and certainly easiest.

When he came away he could not feel that he had much advanced himself.

It was fair-day in the village. Mr. Duffin made his way back to the rectory through cows and pigs and goats innumerable.

The pigs made a noisy corner; they were never still, and were constantly being pursued with shouts, and at a touch of the stick they squealed lustily. The cows for the most part stood patiently, with drooping heads and an absent, far-away look in their soft brown eyes. Sometimes a young heifer lowered her horns to dunch pettishly when she found herself too closely pressed upon.

Outside the nearest public-house a family party were getting into their cart; the bright red shawl of the old woman caught Mr. Duffin's eye as she climbed into the cart and settled herself down beside a couple of discontented pigs, evidently new purchases, and shrieking in agony at being borne off from the friends of their youth.

Mr. Duffin recognised the man who made his way to the horse's head none too steadily, and realised that they had good cause to lament, in that their hours were numbered.

Just beyond the cart a man was vehemently vaunting the milking powers of a melancholy old cow with projecting bones to an indifferent group of possible purchasers.

"Four pounds; not a penny less, barring a shilling or two for luck. Would you have me lose by her? and she such a good milker, and worth every penny of six. Just *look* at her; I axe you to *look* at her!"

Mr. Duffin brushed past the group unheeding.

There had been a sprinkling of rain in the early morning, and the trampling of cattle had worked the dust into mud. Every here and there a little island of egg-shells marked the door of a house of entertainment.

Mr. Duffin had to walk in the road, as the pathway on each side was lined with stalls—stalls for meat, for cheap jewellery, for "dulse" and "yellow man," and round these the school children and their elder sisters gathered.

It was at one of these stalls, on a day just like this, that he had first noticed Ellen Lindsay—yes, just opposite to where that man was auctioning old clothes with immense rapidity and much wit, to judge by the laughter round him.

Mr. Duffin pushed on, gathering whiffs of bad tobacco and whisky and ether as he went. Here and there people touched their hats to him as he passed. One man, who was exceedingly drunk, was full of a desire to "have a crack with his reverence," and to impart to him his views upon the Book of Daniel.

When he had shaken him off, and had got farther on to where the cries of the old clothesman merged in the thin quaver of a flute, Eccles Lindsay, flushed and staggering, was in the midst of a hot dispute with some men from the mountains— queer, shaggy little creatures, with tempers as hot as fire. A plain, showily dressed young woman hung on Eccles' arm, and made an occasional remonstrance. Mr. Duffin caught himself noticing the young man's broad shoulders and strong build.

Before he reached his own gate the crowd thinned and dwindled to an occasional passer-by who had made his purchases early and was taking them home.

Old Mary Ann, sitting in the ditch with her dogs round her, and singing away cheerfully, rose to greet him with her old-fashioned curtsey.

He threw her a careless good morning.

Old Mary Ann responded in her cheerful, shrill tones.

"Och, then, dear, sure it's morning for your reverence and evening for me—the Lord be praised. I was just calling up with your reverence, and ould Betty bid me wait till you would be in."

"You mustn't come so often."

"Troth, I'm sorry it's too often for your reverence. I'd be blithe to come and see your bonny face if I never got a ha'porth. It's not much an old body the like of me needs, and you'd wonder how sensible the childer are, and how they can take the good with the bad. And Charlie's that ould-fashioned he can aye make out something for himself."

Mr. Duffin restrained himself from saying that when her dogs were gone she would find it easier to live. He could not find it in his heart to break the unconscious content of the gay old woman.

In return for a sixpence she called down showers of blessings upon his head, and gave a promise of "stirabout to their supper" to Charlie and the rest.

Mr. Duffin could hear her singing "The Bogie Man" to them as he walked away.

He went into his house quietly, anxious to avoid Betty's society, and sat himself down to the sermon he had left in despair that morning. But again words failed him. This was Saturday, and it must be written; but how could he write when always between him and the paper came Ellen's fair little face and sad blue eyes?

What a merry little thing she had been when he first knew her!

Why, even at Sunday-school, the least thing would touch Ellen's risible faculties, and at treats and festivals she kept all the rest amused.

And what a hero—what a great, glorious being he was in her eyes! How differently he appeared to her and Miss Baring! But Miss Baring was a lady and Ellen was a labourer's daughter.

He tried to draw himself back to his sermon, but he could not find a text to please him; those he came upon seemed too glaringly apposite.

Mr. Duffin had an instinct of considering everything with regard to his own personality. When he had preached of the equality of mankind, it had been with a distinct recollection of the Barings and himself; when of repentance, with a comfortable feeling that his sins were less glaring than those of most men; when he drew vivid pictures of death and the judgment, painting a very fiery, substantial hell, it had been with the conviction that a well-conducted, decorous man like himself was assuredly "saved."

His was distinctly the religion of fear. If he could have put thought behind him his conscience could have been deadened, and his wrong to Ellen have soon been forgotten. But when he had to sit there alone, hour after hour, concentrating his mind in finding words to warn others to turn from sin, his own sermons terrified him in the loneliness.

The temptation had been so strong; Ellen had been so pretty, so sweet, so admiring.

Her yesterday's resistance had roused some of the freshness of his feeling for her, and he could not put her misery out of his head. He had not thought she would take it so hard; he had not, in fact, thought about her at all.

He was uneasy, too. What a fool he had been! Discovery spelt ruin to him; and though she had made no complaint, would she keep silence later on? And when her brothers found out?

Mr. Duffin was not a physical coward, but as he sat there with his sermon Ellen's terror of her brothers began to infect him.

Betty's entrance just then and her words for a moment totally unnerved him.

"Your reverence, Eccles and Wully Lindsay are wanting to see you."

In a pause of silence Mr. Duffin believed that what he dreaded had come, and stared at Betty with white, stricken face.

"I am thinking Eccles and Nancy Jane Dougherty have come to give in their names," the unconscious Betty ended with a giggle.

CHAPTER IX

It had been a long, dreary day — a regular October day, with the sky hidden in thick grey clouds, and an oppression in the air which meant rain in the future. The lake lay dull and leaden behind the poplars, and there were no bright colours in the bog.

Ellen felt herself weighed down and depressed almost beyond endurance. For a time she sat over the fire doing nothing, not thinking definitely of anything. Every now and then she raised her hand to wipe away a slow tear without disturbing her attitude of depressed patience.

When the necessity of feeding the pigs had roused her she wandered listlessly down to her grandmother's cottage, where she found Mrs. Mawhinney and Miss M'Fadden in hot dispute, a circumstance by no means uncommon.

It had begun in the usual way, with Miss M'Fadden's insistence on her right-of-way to the well past her neighbour's door, and perhaps the weather had lent a little extra acerbity to Mrs. Mawhinney's never very sweet temper.

Miss M'Fadden had put down her cans, and stood, her arms akimbo, a provokingly good-natured smile on her fat face. In contrast to the neatness of her enemy, she was, as usual, bursting out of her clothes in all directions; a hastily arranged and very dirty shawl was supposed to conceal the deficiencies of her bodice, but could not hide the gaping interval before her skirt began, nor the long rent which framed a too brief flannel petticoat.

Mrs. Mawhinney was much excited, and declaimed in fury—

"I look for no better from the like of you! To try and desthroy her character—to put your dirty lying insults on her name—may the curse of Heaven light on them that bring themselves to say the like——"

Mrs. Mawhinney broke down into the breathless sobbing of an old woman, and Ellen came forward with a white face.

"What is it, grandma?"

"I'm that put about I hardly know what I'm saying," Mrs. Mawhinney wailed. "To think of the lies I've had to stand——"

"It's the truth I'm telling you," said Miss M'Fadden, still good-humoured. "Sure, we all have our wee failings—they're lifeless that's faultless—and if she did make a slip in her day——"

"I won't listen to it!" Mrs. Mawhinney sobbed. "The like of you, Jane M'Fadden, to dar' to take away the character of a Royal Queen—to dar' to say that Queen Elizabeth would go to meet her lovers in the moonlight——"

"Well, well, well," said Miss M'Fadden leniently, "she was one of them sperity ones——"

Neither of the two would allow her opponent time to finish a sentence. Mrs. Mawhinney broke in indignantly—

"She was one knew how to conduct herself

proper. You may well speak, Jane M'Fadden, when that black divil Parnell———."

Miss M'Fadden in her turn flamed up.

"You're ready enough to cast a stone at a dead man. He's gone to be judged by higher than you or I. He's in the Lord's hands, and it may be that the tears of Ireland will be fit to wash away his sin."

Ellen stood silently, regaining her colour in the relief of finding that it was Queen Elizabeth who was attacked.

The faintest beginning of a breeze rustled the poplars and came to blow about her fair hair, bringing in its train a strong whiff of flax-water.

Her grandmother turned upon her sharply, and asked her what she was standing there glowering for, and Ellen put in her usual plea of "a sore head," which stood for a sore heart.

"She could not thole the pain," she said, imagining that Miss M'Fadden's eyes studied her curiously, and with a word or two she wandered away again restlessly.

"It passes me what ails the wean," Mrs. Mawhinney said, looking after her.

Miss M'Fadden took up her cans in silence; she had her ideas.

All the neighbours had; a wave of gossip had reached all except her own people, and Ellen herself was dimly suspicious that this was so.

In the long, slow-passing days, when the turf was in and there was not much to do, she began to avoid people as well as she could.

She tried her hardest to be like herself, never venturing to look ahead, but fighting desperately from day to day to keep her secret. She felt her father watched her with anxiety; he asked her what ailed her once or twice, and once she heard him say to Eccles, "The wean's not herself."

To cheer her up they tried to devise little pleasures and outings for her, which cut her to the heart. Even Willy disturbed himself about her, and took some trouble to get her a canary, which, he said, would "keep her in company."

A faint rumour of a rumour reached her grandmother at last, and she spoke to Ellen about it one evening.

"Ellen, I've been hearing some unpleasant talk, but I don't doubt it's all lies."

Ellen, with a quick start, braced herself for denial.

"Just that there's a sough that you're not as careful as you might be."

"It's a black lie," said Ellen breathlessly.

"I'm glad of it. A young woman can't mind herself too well. There's nothing of it? There's no one after you?"

"No one," said Ellen; "it's a wicked lie."

Why had she denied it? What was the use? she thought to herself as she walked up the lane. It only meant that she could hold up her head as an honest girl such a little time longer. But that was worth much; it was worth everything to her, for it was all she had left.

The hunted, defiant look in her eyes made her father say at once what had been in his mind for some time.

"I'm afeared you're fretting about not getting to service—is that it, daughter?"

Ellen drew a long, sobbing breath.

"Why, what ails you this minute?" said her father quickly.

"I came too hard up the loanan," said Ellen softly.

CHAPTER X

On Eccles Lindsay's wedding-day the church was crowded. Not his friends only but the whole village had turned out for the occasion, and gossip ran furious.

His life had been a reproduction in another class of that of "a man about town," with the reputation among mothers of being dangerous and not likely to marry. If a girl began to "walk" with Eccles her neighbours predicted misfortune.

Consequently his marriage excited general interest, increased by the knowledge that he had made several efforts to escape it.

Miss M'Fadden sat on a hillock in the churchyard, and as she was known to have all the gossip of the country-side in her head, a group had collected round her. She was gracefully attired in a grey serge skirt, on which she had hastily arranged a flounce with black pins, an old blue satin tea-jacket of Mrs. Baring's, with its glories half concealed by a black velvet cape trimmed with cream lace, and a white straw hat adorned with black satin ribbon and very dilapidated ostrich feathers.

She had all the confidence of feeling herself dressed suitably and well.

"Keep us, Jane! are you going to turn, that

you're coming to a Protestant wedding?" said a jocund neighbour.

"Ne'er a bit of me," said Miss M'Fadden cheerfully; "but I was up at the manor-house with a blouse of Miss Nelly's, and I thought I'd look in and see what sport was going, and show my fine clothes." Here Miss M'Fadden laughed so heartily that she was unable for some minutes to go on. "I'll be on the safe side and not go into the church, but maybe I'm old enough to risk going as far as the porch."

"Would you be surprised, now, to find there was no wedden and Eccles was away to America?"

"Ay, that I would. She has a better hoult of him than that."

The reference was to Nancy Jane Dougherty, who was popularly supposed to have done more than her share to bring about the marriage.

Mr. Johnston, the shoemaker, shook his head wisely.

"He's a slippery one; sure, he'd never have had her if she had not taken a chance when he'd had a glass."

"And maybe you've heard that next week he went to see and get their names off—he and Wully."

"He didn't!" in a tone of much astonishment and interest.

"Sure enough. And Mr. Duffin says if he'd changed his mind, of coorse he couldn't hinder it, and he'd take the names off. And then he sees Eccles and Wully look at one another, and says he, 'What is it now?' And says Eccles, 'But what about the shilling I give in?' 'Sure, I can't give that back,' says Mr. Duffin. And then Eccles looks at Wully, and looks back at

Mr. Duffin, and says he, 'Well, maybe, if that's the way of it, the names had as well stand.'"

"Well, she's getting a careful man any way," said the jocund neighbour.

"But he was off to leave the country after that," said Mr. Johnston.

Miss M'Fadden looked wise.

"No one knows the rights of that," she said, implying that she knew much, did she choose to tell.

"He was clean gone for two days anyhow," said the sexton's wife; "and one day, when we were all saying he be to have gone to New York, Nancy Jane druv off on a car to Ballymagra, and fetched him back dead drunk after daily-goin'. That's the truth, I know, for I saw them getting him into her sister's."

Everybody gave a word of assent. It was well known that Nancy Jane had come to stay with her sister and arranged to have the wedding in Eccles' parish instead of hers by way of making things secure.

"Nancy Jane's not easy daunted," said some one else, and there was a general laugh.

"I don't envy her an unwilling man," said Essie Dawson, who was popularly supposed to have looked on Eccles with eyes of favour.

"Willing or unwilling, they're none so easy to get," said Johnston.

A beginning of stir outside the graveyard broke up the group, not unwillingly, as there was a decided chilliness in the air. For short intervals gleams of cold sunshine burst their way between the clouds, but brought brightness and not heat with them.

Ellen Lindsay came up, separating from her

father at the gate, and gravitating naturally to the women.

She had come out in reckless mood, determined for this last time to throw thought and care to the winds. She *would* forget and enjoy herself.

"Well, daughter, is that you?" said Miss M'Fadden. "Why didn't you put on your jacket? You're that happed up; let me fix the shawl for you."

Ellen drew back.

"I'll do well enough," she said; "I'm cold-rife these days."

"Maybe you're wise," said Miss M'Fadden. "Is there any word of the bride yet? Is it to Ballymagra you're going?"

"It's out that way, and across by Ballysilly," said Ellen.

"Eccles is the boy to choose a road with plenty of publics," said Johnston.

"And Mr. Duffin aye at him to take the pledge."

"He wouldn't till after the wedden; he was keeping himself for that," said Ellen. It was so much a matter of course that every man should get drunk on his wedding-day; to refrain would have been looked on as the evidence of rather a mean spirit.

A distant cheer announced the approach of the wedding party.

Eccles had had "a drop" already, perhaps to screw his courage to the sticking-point. His bride conducted him along firmly, heedless of the ironical cheers with which they were greeted.

Eccles kept glancing suspiciously from side to side, quite aware that he was likely to get a warm reception; but the time had not come yet.

F

The women were rather impressed with the bridal party.

"I can see there's two cars waiting at the least," said the sexton's wife.

"There's no stint, any way. Look at Nancy Jane's dress with *that* deep of satin on it, and good satin, too," said Miss M'Fadden; "and the flowers in her bonnet and a tulle veil, no less! And the sash on her sister wasn't got for nothing."

These details naturally appealed to a dressmaker's soul. She was distressed that Ellen did not represent their side of the lake equally gorgeously.

"I wouldn't like them fereigners to have the crow."

Ellen laughed uncertainly.

"You'll set my *face* before Nancy Jane's at the least," she said.

Nancy Jane was indeed peculiarly plain, but the remark was not like Ellen.

The people crowded into church, anxious to miss nothing. Ellen went with the rest, and whispered and laughed more than any one. Only she carefully kept her eyes from wandering in the direction of the Communion table, where Mr. Duffin stood in his surplice. She had never seen him in church since——

Ellen had no very romantic ideas in connection with matrimony; in her class girls seldom married young, and marriages were for the most part decidedly mercenary, taking "fortune" into first consideration, and next the man's capability of earning, and the woman's strength and housekeeping powers. And this was a particularly unromantic wedding.

Nevertheless she felt it necessary to distract

her mind from the service, which she told herself she would never hear in Nancy Jane's place.

Mr. Duffin, for his part, kept his eyes fastened on his prayer-book, and read hastily and mechanically. Once he had to pause to rebuke the unusual tittering and whispering.

Just before the end of the service his eyes and Ellen's met. They had carefully avoided this, and it was as if a common impulse made their resolution break down at the same moment.

Mr. Duffin saw a sweet little flushed face, with strange, shining eyes. Ellen saw—God knows what sublimated vision of the real man.

She looked down again at once, colouring vividly. She had a curious momentary flash of pride in the knowledge of the link between her and him. But with the look all her false gaiety died out, and left her dazed and troubled.

A few minutes later everything was over. Eccles' head had been gradually clearing during the ceremony. After a pause, to make sure that the last word had been said, he turned abruptly on his heel and made for the church door, leaving his bride to follow as she could.

He had hoped with the suddenness of his retreat to cut his way through the group of his contemporaries at the door, from which he knew what to expect, and he almost succeeded. One storm of rice and flour did reach him before he was out of the church; the rest he escaped. A slipper, which Miss M'Fadden had been carefully preserving, caught the best man on the side of the head, and the bride and best maid had their dresses whitened with flour.

Eccles waited for nothing; by the time the rest of the party were out of church he was to be seen making his way at racing speed over the fields.

The bride took the matter with commendable calmness. She remarked that Eccles " be to have disremembered about setting down their names, but maybe it wouldn't make much odds," and that " they'd better be starting, and they'd likely meet him a piece down the road." She seemed much more disturbed about the damage to her dress than about her bridegroom's behaviour and the excitement round her.

There was a confusion over the start. Ellen had only to hold back a little and allow a younger Dougherty girl, in high delight, to take her place on the second car. There was no time for discussion, and the horses were cold and frightened by the noise, and would not stand.

The cars went off at a hand-gallop amidst deafening cheers and not a little hooting, and the whole party swept down the road after them.

Ellen was left in the graveyard alone. More and more in the distance she could hear cries of " A wedden! a wedden!" in the shrill voices of children who were just out of school. She shivered in the cold wind, which was stripping the trees in gusts and making little heaps of the dead leaves which fell every now and then with a swish at her feet.

Mr. Duffin came hastily out of the vestry.

" I was afraid you wouldn't wait," he said. He faced Ellen with quivering lips and passionate eyes.

She made no answer in words; her whole expression and attitude answered. What did it matter? What difference could it make now?

"Ellen, is there anything I can do? Can't I help you?"

She shook her head indifferently.

"If—if—you see that there's no good—no good at all in my speaking out——"

Mr. Duffin, crimson, stammered and paused. He was trying to compromise and convince his own conscience, while at the same time to put into words a difficult request for Ellen's silence. It was a promise which he found it very hard to ask for, and yet it was so necessary, so very necessary that he should get it.

Ellen looked at him uncomprehendingly.

"What I mean is——" In the difficulty of expressing his meaning he caught eagerly at any excuse for postponing it. "Why, child," he said, "you are shaking."

"It's with the cold," said Ellen.

The wind was coming in increasing gusts round the corner of the church, bearing with it a sprinkling of ice-cold rain. In the distance they could still hear a vague sound of cheering and catch a last glimpse of the two cars at a hill on the road.

"Come—come into the vestry," said Mr. Duffin in an impulse.

He drew her into the warmth with him. The little room looked cosy; there was a good fire in the grate, and a crimson cloth on the table that held his prayer-book and a glass and bottle of water.

Ellen stood where he left her with the warmth gradually creeping into her chilled little figure.

He looked at her for a moment.

"Don't look so wretched," he said. "Do you think I've no feeling? You make me miserable."

"I'm very sorry, sir. You'd better let me go home."

"But there's this — if you're wanting money——"

"Money's little use when you're heart-broke," said Ellen in a hard voice.

Her quiet apathy disturbed him more than tears or protestations.

He shifted his feet uncomfortably and tapped on the table.

Ellen had not lost her prettiness; her face had even gained in a delicacy which Mr. Duffin, curiously, found particularly attractive.

All morning he had had burning in his mind the fact that the Barings were having a party, and had not asked him, and the remembrance of his embarrassing out-of-placeness at the Lawsons' the afternoon before.

A thought that had already come into his mind once or twice flashed back again. Why not ease his conscience—end this lonely life—make himself safe? Ellen was as sweet and dainty as any lady, and in another parish——

They two were together, completely alone, shut in to a warmth and comfort which went to his head like intoxication. The rain drove sharply against the window, bringing with it a stray leaf which tapped so humanly against the glass that he started.

Ellen stood looking into the fire with the face of one who expected nothing more of life. The temptation to bring the old sparkle to her eyes and the old smile to her lips overcame him.

He filled a glass of water and drained it. Then he drew close to her and let his hand fall warmly on hers.

"Ellen," he said hoarsely. His voice, breaking the silence, sounded strange to himself. "Ellen—shall we be married?"

The words were said—half against his own will and intention they were said.

Ellen turned on him in a flash.

"Oh!" she said breathlessly, "oh——"

"I mean it—I swear to you——"

She caught him up passionately.

"Mind what you say—mind what you say! I'm—I'm not sure that I rightly understand——"

"I am going to marry you." As Mr. Duffin repeated the words they seemed all at once unbearably compromising and ruinous and unnecessary.

Ellen's whole face was drawn together in an effort to be quite sure.

"Say it again slow? I've maybe took you up wrong. Did you say you would be willin'—to—marry me?"

"Yes."

She turned such a ghastly white that for a moment he thought she was going to faint; but instead she burst into a very storm of weeping.

CHAPTER XI

Independent Heroes' L.O.L., No. 177.
M'Cance's True-Blues, L.O.L., No. 320.

A Soiree and Ball in Connection with above Lodges
will be held in
BALLYTURBET ORANGE HALL,
On Thursday Evening, 8th December.

Tea on the Table at 7 o'clock.

Wreaths of Orange, Blue, and Purple
   Our most glorious ball do grace;
Maids so spotless as the turtle,
   Hail your welcome to our place.

Dear brethren, we you invite
   While our golden lamp doth shine;
Spreading lustre all around,
   With beams of light almost divine.

And ladies, too, we call on you
   Our joys and pleasures for to share,
And Ballyturbet boys, who fear no noise,
   Will rejoice to meet you there.

Admission (Gentlemen) .... One Shilling.

This legend engraved on a bright orange card, and with the addition of a list of stewards and a picture of King William on a prancing steed was presented to Miss M'Fadden across her open half-door as an excellent joke, and by her received with much amusement.

It was not often that "Black Wully" condescended to any lightness in his dealing with "Papists," and marked a state of great good-humour on his part. But his jokes were always of a somewhat grim kind and not to be trifled with. Had Barclay not been crippled the present one might not improbably have ended in rough words at the best.

But Miss M'Fadden, who was doing her hair after a perfunctory fashion at a glass by the bed, received him with hearty laughter.

"Get away with you, Wully; you might have more sense."

"Sense, indade! when I'm after inviting you to take the flure with me. Sure, don't I show my sense in choosing the likeliest young woman hereabout?"

Willy Lindsay stood lounging in the doorway after a half-stooped, slouching fashion which hid his real height, but could not hide his broad shoulders and strongly knit form. His coarse, black hair framed a large face with prominent cheek-bones, small, deep-set eyes, and small, very white teeth—an ignorant, cruel face, the face of a low type of Irish Celt.

"You ought to have seen me a while ago," said Miss M'Fadden jovially, "painting away for dear life at a flag for the seventeenth, and setting between a window open at the one side and the dure at the other to make the paint dry quick, with Barclay grumbling at the draught."

"Heth! I didn't know you were a painter," said Willy.

"Sure, she'd make an offer at anything," Barclay commented from his bed.

"And why not? Who knows what they can do till they try? And when I heard the boys talking in trouble over the expense of a new flag, I up and says I could maybe get a bit of white satin from an old ball-dress of Miss Nelly's, and if they'd give me a pot of paint and a pictur' of Emmet they should have the best flag they iver had."

"She's not easy beat," Barclay said, after his usual fashion of indulgent approval.

"I'll hould you'd like a sight of it, Wully? The white satin, with Emmet's blue coat and his cheeks like roses, is just the purtiest thing you ever seen. And there's not many would have done it as well at the first set off, forby having to pull out the hairs of my head to make a brush with."

Miss M'Fadden made no attempt to conceal her pride, and Willy did not fail to make some approving comments.

"You'll maybe paint us a flag for the twelfth?" he said.

"Maybe I will," said Miss M'Fadden. "I'm thinking, if I get time, I'll paint a few pictur's to lighten up the wall while my hand's in. But I've that blouse of Miss Nelly's to finish first. Where did I lay it, Barclay? You had it to cover you last night, and I haven't seen it since."

It was perhaps as well for Miss Baring's peace of mind that she did not know all the vicissitudes through which her clothes passed.

This particular blouse was in due time unearthed from under the bed, and Miss M'Fadden set to work with her machine to use up the remains of daylight.

"Miss Nelly is set on having it by Tuesday," she explained to Willy, "and she's a fancy to have made it in some way of her own, and nothing else will do her. To my eye all them colours look just washed out, but the quality have their queer fancies; and indeed, as I told Miss Nelly when she showed me the stuff, it's that odd you might say it was pretty through ugliness."

Willy took himself off with a curt nod before the whizz of the machine began. Two of the M'Cances were going to America, he said, and he was going to the "convoy" to-night, but he had to be in Ballyturbet, to an Orange meeting, first.

"And I'll hould there'll be plenty of whisky going at the 'convoy,' and Wully won't come off with less than his share," Miss M'Fadden stopped her machine for a moment to say.

"And him only just getting to his work again after Eccles' wedden," said Barclay.

"Heth! there wasn't a boy fit to walk home *that* evening," said Miss M'Fadden, with a laugh; "and the sough says Nancy Jane had had as much as was good for her. But since then she has made Eccles take the pledge, and I'm tould she says she'll tache him with a stick if he ever comes home to her in drink."

"I'm not envying Eccles, fortune and all," said Barclay.

Then came a silence, in which nothing but the whirr of the machine was to be heard.

Barclay lay still, his eyes dreamily wandering about the cottage.

The noise of the machine sometimes drove him beyond endurance, and then his sister had to stop it for a time, but he always bore as long as he could. It meant meat and drink to them both.

He lay, as he had lain so many evenings, watching the dusk gradually creeping over the bog; he liked to see the crimson band of sunset growing narrower, while the bright colours scattered over the turf merged by degrees into a misty brown.

When the Lindsays' cottage ceased to be distinct he called to his sister.

"It's time for you to leave working and wet the tea," he said; "sure, you can't see what you're at."

"It's early dark this evening."

"No earlier than usual. I can tell by the time Ellen Lindsay goes for the goats; she's just gone by this minute."

"I never see Ellen go out till daily-goin' these days," said Miss M'Fadden. "I hope all's right with the wean; I'd be loath for anything to ail her. But she's been aye left too much her lone."

Barclay made no answer, and his sister began obediently to get ready tea. Then she crossed the kitchen to close the half-door, and paused, looking out into the dusk.

Ellen came up the lane, leading the grey goat by its tether, and singing softly to herself as she came. She stopped when she saw Miss M'Fadden at her door, turning to her with a sudden smile.

Miss M'Fadden greeted her favourite cheerily.

"Is that you, daughter? Heth! it's a long time since I heard you singing. You're light-hearted this evening."

"I am that," said Ellen, with a quiver in her voice.

"You're mended quarely this last while, but you're not back to yourself."

"Oh, I'm rightly."

Ellen paused still, and the grey goat began to crop grass by the side of the lane. She did not know exactly what she was waiting for, nor try to analyse why it was a comfort to be near fat, good-natured Miss M'Fadden. The girl had missed her mother in a thousand practical ways all her life, but never as she did now. It seemed so forlornly lonely that all should go on as usual, everybody remain placid and unmoved, while she was living every hour in intense excitement. She would have died rather than speak out one of the thousand hopes and fears bursting through her mind, but she wanted another woman to understand and sympathise by instinct.

Yet she shrank at once into herself at something more than usually kind in Miss M'Fadden's voice when she asked her to "come in and lain down a while."

"What! with the goat?" said Ellen, with a laugh. "She nearly has the arms pulled out of me as it is. Dear! but these dark evenings make the time from daily-goin' ill to pass. I just keep wishing for the next morning, the days are that long."

There was a world of restlessness in her voice.

"I'm going to Ballymagra the morrow morn," she said. She could not help saying it; though how was Miss M'Fadden to know what going to Ballymagra meant to Ellen?

"Are you, indade? That's a long road, and you none that strong."

"Oh, I'm strong enough. You're fit to do a deal when your heart's light," said Ellen, with a sigh cut short.

Was her heart so very light?

As she began to shorten the goat's tether with

a view to moving on, a little bent figure drew out of the dusk, coming towards the cottage in a line which was by no means of the straightest.

"Sure, it's old Mary," said Miss M'Fadden. "You're just in time for a drop of tea—why, what ails you, woman?"

Old Mary Ann crawled into the cottage and let herself drop wearily on a stool by the fire. She seemed to have shrunk into herself and grown smaller and browner than ever, and she volunteered neither word nor blessing.

"What ails you?" Miss M'Fadden repeated.

"They've took them away."

"What is it they've took, dear? Would it be your childer? Is that what you're maning? Did anything happen them?"

"Ay, they took them away. They drownded the puppies and took the rest. They were harming nobody, but there wasn't one to speak for me."

Miss M'Fadden flamed up indignantly.

"It's a dirty, mean shame! The divil fly away with them that done it! We'll make them give them back, darlint, never fear. Wait till I give the fire a stir; you're just bate out with the cold. Sure, we'll spake to his honour or Mr. Duffin."

"Yes, I'll warrant they'll help you," said Ellen eagerly.

"It's no use," said old Mary Ann wearily; "the puppies are drownded. I followed after, and I could hear them squealin' as they felt the water. And you wouldn't believe how petted they were on me and how knowing they'd got. I've took a drop since, that I don't deny; I couldn't thole to mind it."

Ellen suddenly covered her face with her hands,

"Oh," she said, "it's dreadful to see any one unhappy!"

Miss M'Fadden had gone to the dresser for a candle. When she turned round again the girl had disappeared into the darkness.

Miss M'Fadden shook her head dubiously.

"I hope all's right with the wean," she said again.

CHAPTER XII

ELLEN was up long before daybreak the next morning. She dressed herself by the light of a candle, and though she moved as softly as she could, her father woke, and grumbled at being roused so early these dark days. What did Ellen want in Ballymagra at all, and why need she be there so early?

She could hardly concentrate her attention sufficiently to give intelligible answers.

She was to meet Mr. Duffin at the registry office at ten o'clock, and she must leave herself two good hours for the walk.

But she was quite ready soon after half-past seven; she had fed the chickens and milked the goats, and given her father his breakfast, though she had scarcely tasted her own. Just as well to be on the safe side and start a little early; she would then be sure to get away before the neighbours were about, and she felt as if all who saw her *must* guess her errand. Besides, who knew what delays she might meet with?

When she opened the door the cold morning air rushed in, and she paused a moment on the threshold, looking back at her unconscious father, who was lighting his pipe.

"Have you everything to your hand, da?

You'll find a piece of bacon on the second shelf of the dresser, and if I'm not in to milk the goats by evening——"

Lindsay stared at her.

"Keep us! Sure, you'll be in by then if you're ever coming!"

Ellen still made a wistful pause. When she saw her father knock the ashes out of his pipe and prepare to go out she turned away slowly.

There was a red line of faintest coming sunrise across the lake as she started, and her feet went over the grass, damp with heavy dew, with a squelching sound. When her shawl brushed the hedge it brought back a sprinkling of tiny dewdrops.

She got her hands wet and scratched gathering a spray of yellow whin blossom to pin in her shawl.

The damp morning air exhilarated her. She was painfully excited now that the culminating moment had almost come. She had not realised before how the anxiety of the last few weeks had weighed upon her nerves. Now, she told herself, all *must* be well.

Marriage would make all right. "A slip" was not regarded severely if the man "made an honest woman" of the girl he had betrayed.

These were the sentiments and opinions of her neighbours, and Ellen was not beyond them. She felt that the approaching ceremony in the registry office would lift the largest portion of shame from her shoulders and make her very happy.

Who would dare to say a word against the minister's wife, who would live at the rectory and have a servant to do her bidding? How proud her father would be! He need never do another hand's turn unless he chose. Ellen had very happy, wonderful dreams, into which Mr. Duffin's figure came with a kind of awed worship. Was it within the limits of possibility that some day she would be asked "to her dinner" at the manor-house? Nothing seemed impossible in this marvellous new world which was before her—a glorious prospect to Ellen.

But it never occurred to her that Mr. Duffin might wish to take her away from Ballyturbet.

The future after ten o'clock that day was vague and dream-like.

She had only seen Mr. Duffin once since the day of Eccles' marriage, and he had told her nothing but the time and place where she was to meet him.

The light grew every moment clearer as she walked. She scarcely felt the five long Irish miles. Her mind was so far away that once an early bread-cart nearly ran her down.

As she drew near Ballymagra she became seized with a fear that she might be late, and hurried on feverishly till her breath went. The clock at home might be wrong, or she might have been slower than she had thought.

She only slackened her pace when she came in sight of the church clock at Ballymagra, which told her it was half-past nine.

She was too early after all, and she might have known it, as Mr. Duffin had not overtaken her.

She sat down by the roadside to wait, but the grass was damp still, and she felt as if all eyes were upon her. It was as if her story was written in her face for passers-by to read.

Meeting the curious glance of a girl driving three skinny cows, Ellen got up and wandered a little way down the road. But the clock drew her back.

A quarter, ten minutes to ten. Perhaps she had better go on to the registry office and wait about there.

It was a neat little box of a house, with a scrap of avenue and a garden.

Ellen lingered outside the gate, wondering if by any chance she could have missed Mr. Duffin.

She could not bring herself to ask any questions; it seemed to her as if to do so would be to betray all. She became self-conscious to agony, crimsoning under the careless glance of passers-by.

When the clock struck ten she gained courage to stop a small boy and ask him if there was any other road from Ballyturbet. The boy stared at her and said he did not know. He was late for school and would not wait to think.

Ellen was discouraged, and made no attempt to stop any one else.

Once a woman paused and asked if aught ailed her, but Ellen's answer was so abrupt in her alarm that she turned away offended.

What could have happened?

Half-an-hour later an idea occurred to her: perhaps Mr. Duffin had been before her, and was waiting for her all this time in the registry office.

This possibility gave her courage to make her way very slowly, and with much hesitation, to the little house.

A red-haired boy came to answer her knock. Ellen could hardly find breath or words.

She said, "There isn't a gentleman waiting here, sir?"

And when the boy said there was no one, she asked desperately for Mr. Duffin by name.

"There's nobody called yet," said the boy consolingly, "but likely he'll be in later."

Ellen turned away and walked slowly down the avenue.

"It's naught but that he's been kept," she said to herself resolutely; "it's not easy for the like of him to get away."

She did not like to wait near the house lest she should be noticed, but she could not bring herself to go far away. Besides, she was beginning to feel very tired, and ill and weak from want of food.

Every now and then she walked a little way up the road, sitting down to rest occasionally. It was a cold, grey day, with thick clouds, and Ellen found her shawl scarcely enough protection.

She resolutely kept her mind a blank, not allowing distinct form to an awful fear that hung over her.

About twelve o'clock she again ventured to the registry office, on the wild chance that Mr. Duffin might have passed in unnoticed by her.

The boy was fairly sympathetic—too sympathetic for Ellen's comfort. She knew he was looking after her as she went down the path.

By this time she was too worn-out and feeling too ill to walk any more. She went to a little distance from the office and sat down drearily by the hedge. The grey clouds were resolving themselves into rain, which came first in a few slow drops, and increased to a steady downpour.

Ellen's light shawl was soon wet through, but she never thought of seeking shelter. Her mind could not get beyond the one fixed idea of waiting there for Mr. Duffin. He had been detained, but he *must* come; it was impossible that he would not come.

A good-natured postman paused on his round to advise the girl to seek shelter. Ellen felt a difficulty in keeping her voice from breaking into a scream as she sought for words to answer him. When he saw she was obstinate he went on and left her.

She could feel little streams of water running down her neck, and her feet rested in a puddle; but she was apathetically indifferent, and hardly noticed discomfort or hunger.

Every time she heard wheels, or even footfalls, she was on her feet with strained eyes. When the early dusk of a December day began to creep on she was still waiting.

There had been very few passers-by for the last hour or so. It was some time since Ellen had even had a chance of hoping, when she suddenly caught sight of the dark figure of a man in the distance.

He was coming along the wet road after the fashion of one who was tired, splashing through the mud without choosing his steps and stooping in his walk. She had been disappointed so many times that she refused to let herself spring to her feet, and sat still, trembling and waiting.

This time the man did not pass the registrar's gate; he turned into it, and under his umbrella Ellen told herself she recognised Mr. Duffin's figure.

At last!

She forgot wet, weariness, hunger, as she made her way once more to the house.

She could see his footprints up the path; already a tiny puddle was forming where each heel had been.

Her fingers were almost too numb to raise the knocker, and it slipped from her and fell with a bang which resounded through the little house.

This time a woman came to the door—a middle-aged, sharp-faced woman, who looked Ellen suspiciously up and down. But she was past caring.

"I want to see Mr. Duffin," she said.

"You're the young woman my boy was telling me about. There's no Mr. Duffin here that I know of."

"But I saw him go in just now," said Ellen impatiently.

"You saw nothing of the kind. You saw my husband; he's just in to his tea, and if you've nothing more to say I had as lieve go back to mine."

Ellen persisted desperately.

"You must be making a mistake—oh, you must!"

The woman's voice was kinder as she answered. Perhaps she was touched by the youth of the girl's strained white face, weary with hope deferred.

"Were you expecting to meet this Mr. Duffin?" she said.

"Oh yes," said Ellen; "he promised faithful. He will have been in to speak about it; we were to be married to-day."

"Duffin—I'm pretty sure there's no one of the

name of Duffin. But I'll ask my husband. Step into the hall, young woman."

Ellen thanked her stupidly. There was a strong whiff of bacon and eggs in the house, and the registrar—a stout man with a red beard—was munching when he came out. He had had a long day, and was tired and so impatient of the interruption.

"What's all this about, my girl? I've no one of the name of Duffin."

"Maybe he only put my name—Ellen Lindsay. There *must* be some mistake."

"There's no mistake about it. There's no licence for any such marriage been asked for, and in any case it's long after canonical hours. You'd just better go home as fast as you can."

Ellen stood looking at him stupidly, till he repeated his words.

He did so rather impatiently, anxious to go back to his tea. Three or four children were peering out of the open door of the dining-room, with a background of fire and lamplight.

Ellen turned away in silence. There was nothing to be said. She gathered her shawl about her and went out into the rain.

The registrar and the registrar's wife looked at each other, and he shrugged his shoulders.

"She's put off the marriage a trifle too long and he's given her the slip," he said; "some young scamp probably."

"But I am sure she said the *Reverend* Mr. Duffin," said the boy who had answered the door.

"Nonsense! Reverend indeed! A pretty reverend!"

"She looked so ill I half felt I ought to ask her

to rest," said the registrar's wife; "but I'm afraid she's a bad character."

"There's the workhouse near hand. Shut the door, Bob; it's an awful night; and come in to tea—everything will be half cold."

. . . . . .

Ellen began mechanically to walk towards home. The rain drove in her face, but she scarcely felt it. She went on hopelessly, with a miserable ache at her heart which caught her breath.

In her greatest unhappiness before she had had the comfort of extreme youth, the comfort of self-pity, but now her despair was too crushing.

One or two people passed her, indistinct figures in the dusk, and she replied, without thinking what she was saying, to their greeting of "A saft evening."

She was dreadfully tired; so tired that every step was a painful effort, and physical suffering began to take possession of her.

The road, so short in the hopeful morning, seemed endless now. The terrible thought of facing her father made her steps slow at first, but after a time all distinct ideas faded into a longing to get where she could rest.

The possibility of not going home did not occur to her; she was too dazed to think out a plan for herself.

Once or twice she sat down by the roadside, but always gathered herself up again, in the haunting fear that she might find herself unable to get on. A thought that she might die there alone she found unbearable.

Her wet clothes hung on her and weighed her down; her shawl had half slipped from her shoulders and dragged unheeded in the mud. Very soon she found herself staggering from side to side of the road like a drunken woman; once or twice she stumbled and fell, but always dragged herself up again, pursued by her great terror.

She had got beyond caring for anything except to get to the end of this endless road.

On and on and on.

The darkness grew. Ellen was usually afraid of the dark; this evening she scarcely noticed it.

Her feet ached as she dragged them along, and tears, of which she was quite unconscious, were streaming down her face and mingling with the rain.

She seemed to have been walking for years before the freer air told her she had reached the bog. She was nearly home now; she could even see the light from her father's cottage.

The rain fell in a steady sheet into the holes of bog-water, and made running streams down the cart-tracks on the road, through which Ellen splashed drearily. Every step was more difficult, and she stumbled and slipped in the mud.

At last her legs failed her altogether, and she fell in a heap at the side of the road, with her face in a tuft of heather. She tried to rise to her feet, but her knees gave way, and a sharp, terrible pain shook her from head to foot. So near home; it would be dreadful to die out there, all alone, when she was so near.

She gathered all her strength and began to crawl forward on her hands and knees.

Suddenly she sank down with a shrill cry of mortal fear.

.   .   .   .

Lindsay and his eldest son were sitting over the fire in their cottage smoking diligently.

"I wonder Ellen is not back," said the father; "she'll be fairly drookit, and I don't like her being out to this hour."

"Maybe there was some one in from Ballyturbet with a cart, and she waited to get a sail home," Willy suggested.

"The walk's naught to her, but it's terrible dark."

"Maybe I had as well go to the head of the loanan and see if there is a sight of her," said the son, not too eagerly.

As he said it he stooped to pick up a turf to light his pipe, and the door burst open, letting in a gust of rain.

Miss M'Fadden stood on the threshold with a white face.

"Wully! go for the doctor!"

She had run up the lane, and her words came in gasps.

Willy sprang up and reached for his hat.

"What is it? Is Barclay bad?" he said.

"It's not him; it's your Ellen."

Both men faced her in a flash.

"Our Ellen? What's happened her?"

"She's tarrable bad. I'm clean out of my wits since I found her. Run, Wully; there's no time to lose."

Willy waited for no more; he turned and sped out into the darkness.

"Found her?" Lindsay repeated.

"She'd dropped down by the bog. By the goodness of God she let a scraigh out of her as she fell, and I heard it."

"What ails her?"

Lindsay faced Miss M'Fadden sternly, and found his answer in her eyes.

He staggered back, with a grey colour creeping into his face.

"My God!"

CHAPTER XIII

"Dear Mr. Duffin,—Sir William and I will be glad if you will give us the pleasure of your company to dinner on Saturday next at 7.30.—Yours very truly, Emily Lawson."

The writer of this formal note would have been very much surprised if she had known all it was responsible for.

When Mr. Duffin had parted with Ellen Lindsay at the vestry-door more than three weeks before, it had been with no other intention than that of keeping his promise, though he had already begun to have doubts about the advisability of having promised. His idea had been to marry Ellen privately at the registry office at Ballymagra, and then send her away for a time, to be brought in some sort to his conception of a lady, while he made arrangements to transfer himself to another parish.

A remembrance of Ellen's soft blue eyes and a sense of his own surpassing virtue kept him at first from too decided repentance.

He had honestly believed at the time what he told her, that marriage at a registry office necessitated a delay of twenty-one days.

When he discovered that it could be arranged in two he did not feel himself called upon to announce this fact.

But it gave him an excuse for delay; there was plenty of time, and no occasion for haste. There would be sure to be difficulties and complications. His own name was a common one, and he could probably give it as that of one of his parishioners without arousing suspicion, but other awkwardnesses might arise not to be so easily dealt with. In the end he must, of course, put himself in the power of the registrar.

Then he began to wish he had left things alone. He told himself that very likely Ellen had taken matters easily enough, and a present of a new dress and some money would have completely consoled her. Was it his fault that the little fool had not been able to take care of herself? If it had not been him, it would have been some other man. The girl had only drawn back because she wanted to make the best bargain she could, and probably her father knew about it all the time, and was playing his own game. And he, in his kind-heartedness, had allowed himself to be taken in.

Mr. Duffin actually roused himself to indignation against Ellen, while all the time he knew that he was lying to himself.

The one time he and Ellen had met, he had gone with a half intention of telling her she must give up all idea of this ridiculous marriage; but they had parted with the words unsaid.

He *could* not say them, and even the wish to say them vanished when he was with her.

Every day—almost every hour—he vacillated backwards and forwards without ever definitely telling himself that it would be possible to break his word.

In truth, the man suffered. Perhaps it cost

him as much to face giving up the sordid and trivial ambition for which he had borne so long and struggled so hard, as if he had been a nobler man abandoning an infinitely nobler life's desire.

When the house was particularly uncomfortable and Betty extra drunk, he would sink to depths of depression and tell himself that fate was against his ever raising himself, and he might as well marry Ellen and end his unendurable loneliness. But often he thought differently.

On Thursday morning, when he must go to the registry office or be too late, Lady Lawson's note came, and gave him some miserable hours.

He had never been asked to dinner before; it meant—what might it not mean? From how many possibilities was he not about to shut himself out by his quixotism?

He turned upon Betty as she was taking away the breakfast things, and ordered his horse and trap in his "dourest" voice.

But when he was almost ready to start, there came a sick call from the very extremity of his parish—a sick call which he welcomed as a rescue.

He went, and remained a long time, extending his visit to one or two other parishioners in the neighbourhood, and telling himself that duty had made him too late for that day, even had his horse been fit for a further drive.

He could meet Ellen at Ballymagra on Saturday and explain to her the necessity for postponement. She must remember that he was not of her class, and not always free at his own pleasure.

But each hour as it went by left him more unwilling to fulfil his rash promise. The Lawsons' invitation came between him and his rest.

On Saturday morning he woke with the beginning of a heavy cold, which made him still more unwilling for exertion, and was met when he came downstairs with the information that his horse had gone lame.

Betty, who brought him the news, was startled at the grim way he received it.

" He was just travelling up and down the room when I come in and told him," she said to M'Gra, a stout, bandy-legged man, who was coachman, gardener, and general factotum at the rectory, "and he turns on me sharp, and says he, 'Are you maning the horse isn't fit to drive?' And says I, 'Troth, dear, I'm afeard so; but indeed you are as well in, for I'm thinking you have a brash of cold on you.' And he looks at his watch, and says he, 'It's nine o'clock. You might have telt me sooner;' and he mutters something to himself about its being no fault of his. And then, in the middle of my putting him in mind that the Almighty sends such things, he comes at me to 'lave him in pace.' In pace, indade! and he never ceasing to travel up and down like a dog on a chain."

No fault of his. Mr. Duffin might say so to himself and to Betty, but he could not *feel* it. He spent most of the morning pacing his room, occasionally sitting down and trying to concentrate himself on a book; he changed his mind a dozen times an hour.

What was Ellen doing? Of course it would be all right; if she went at all she would soon find he was not there, and turn back, and no harm done. Was it his fault that his horse had gone lame?

He had more time for thought than he desired,

as he could not bring himself to go out, though his sense told him that he was more than unlikely to meet Ellen. He sat over the fire and nursed his cold miserably, almost driven wild by Betty's anxious inquiries for his health every time she entered the room.

In the afternoon he sat with a sheet of sermon-paper in front of him, absolutely idealess. When the rain began to fall he could not keep his eyes from the window. Surely Ellen was at home before this? Of course she would have been told at the registry office that it was too late now for a marriage to take place.

In any case it was not his fault.

But it was his misfortune that he felt himself the meanest cur in creation.

He could not even manage to take the comfort he had hoped for out of the prospect of the Lawsons' dinner.

In the evening, after a severe tussle with Betty, who was inclined to refuse him permission to go out in the wet with his cold, he went to the Lawsons', and found himself face to face with Mr. and Mrs. M'Cune, in whose presence his sense of gratification vanished.

It was entirely a parish entertainment. Sir William Lawson had been for a long time member for his county in the old days when things were very different and there was no ballot, and he had kept up the habit of conciliation long after the rest of the world. And having come of a Presbyterian stock, like all the Northern gentry, he never forgot it. Besides, he personally liked Mr. M'Cune, who was well read and clever, and knew his own place quite as well as Sir William knew his.

All Mr. Duffin's efforts to place himself on a different level from the M'Cunes were wasted; all the condescension in his manner of addressing them was lost upon the Lawsons. It was hard indeed that his evening should be spoilt by the presence of the man of whom in all the world he was most bitterly jealous.

Mr. Duffin ended by subsiding into a disgusted silence; he sat and sniffed till he drove Lady Lawson nearly frantic.

He was a miserably unromantic object as he sat there with his eyes bleared and his nose red with cold, and the suggestion of a sneer on his thick lips whenever Mr. M'Cune spoke.

But, unromantic as he looked, wherever he turned his eyes he had a vision of Ellen Lindsay's white, reproachful face.

The next morning Betty was eager with news; she watched on the stairs for her master to come down to breakfast, and followed him into the dining-room, settling herself in her favourite attitude by the sideboard.

"Ye'll be surprised to hear the news I have this Sabbath morn," she said. "Ellen Lindsay has come to trouble."

Mr. Duffin was pouring out his tea; he started and splashed on the cloth. Then he laid down the tea-pot with his cup half full, and a dull red creeping into his face.

Betty was for the moment diverted to distress about the cloth.

"Just look to it now! And a clean cloth!" she said reproachfully; "and it to do you, the Lord knows how long. Well, I'm aye telling you a man's not fit to live his lane, and it's time you were getting a mistress to see to you, for the

Lord knows it's more than I'm equal to. But, as I was telling you, I still said that Ellen would come to no good—too many gallivantings. Not but what her father was aye a good, releegious, wee man. But I mind——"

"What about—the girl?"

"I mind," Betty went on undisturbed, "there was a far-out friend of hers—Tilly Johnston— had a misfortune and went clean silly. They're saying Ellen tried to drownd herself last night. Her father'll be badly put out; he thought such a dale of her. They say the baby is not the size of a kittling—them bye-blows are mostly wee. It's tarrable, dear, the like of such wickedness; but this is a sinful world, and the original sin——"

"That'll do," said Mr. Duffin hoarsely.

"Even the best outsides," Betty moralised, waving her arm, "are not to be trusted. They're saying the father of the child is that young Archie Kennedy, that's so constant at Sabbath-school, and I suppose they'll be processing him; but if Eccles or Wully get a hoult of him there won't be much call for processing."

"Hold your tongue! You sicken me!" said Mr. Duffin, writhing in his seat.

"And they say Ellen will hardly last through the day," Betty went on, gloating ghoul-like over her scandal, "so they'll likely be sending for your reverence——"

"Great God!"

"And I'm studying to think who they'll have to lay her out. Ellen 'll make a beautiful corpse —there's been no time for her to fail any. Sure your reverence isn't ating any breakfast; it's the heavy cold that's on you. Heth, dear! I've a good mind to send a message to the church that you're not fit to go."

Mr. Duffin pushed his untouched plate away, with but one thought in his mind—to escape from the martyrdom of Betty's tongue.

He allowed her to provide him with a thick muffler and overwhelm him with advice, scarcely conscious of what he was doing.

"And keep this tight up round your throat, dear, and mind to keep your mouth shut when you're in the air," Betty gave her parting instructions, bringing a whiff of whisky whenever she moved.

Mr. Duffin left himself in her hands like a man in a dream.

In church that day, in default of new ideas, he preached an old sermon of his on God's anger with sinners; while, not a mile away, Ellen Lindsay lay fighting for her life.

CHAPTER XIV

"WHAT I say I hold to," said Willy Lindsay in his most ugly tone; "if I have to stan' here to hinder it, Ellen never crosses the dure she's disgraced."

"If she does, with my will neither Nancy Jane nor I ever do," said Eccles, the milder spirit.

The two sons stood together, facing their father, who was sitting by the table, his head leaning on his hand.

"And what is to come of her, then?" he said.

"She may go to the House—or drownd for all I care," said Willy roughly; "if I'd been listened to she'd have gone at once, and if it killed her, no great matter. Instead of which she's been a burden on the M'Faddens, dacent people."

"The House is the right place for the like of her," said Eccles.

Willy gave his sister a very coarse word.

The father rose to his feet suddenly.

"Shame on you, boys!" he said passionately.

He paused, moistening his dry lips and pulling at the scarf round his neck as if it choked him. But when he went on his words came more easily.

"Shame on you for cowards!" he said. "Is it when trouble comes that you turn from them that you couldn't make enough of in their joy?

Is it you, Wully, the worst drunkard through the place, or you, Eccles, with more than one poor lass's ruin on your shoulders—is it you that set yourselves up to judge? The Book tells us to be marciful as we hope for marcy; and would ye crush one that's heart-broke enough without that—a weak wee lass, little beyond a wean, with no mother to see to her—God help her!" He caught his breath, and turned upon his sons with fierce anger—"And may His curse light upon you if you don't draw from your wickedness!"

Lindsay brought his hand down on the table violently and sank back into his seat.

There was an uncomfortable pause. Willy and Eccles looked at each other, awed and silenced.

Presently their father again spoke in a changed, dull voice.

"I'm maybe wrong to speak like that, boys. You've been good sons to me, and sure you're young—and it's natural you should be angered. But my lass must come home. As long as I'm fit to do a hand's turn—as long as I've the strength for a day's labour, and a roof to cover me, she will aye have a welcome by her father's fireside; let them that's naught to her give ill words if they will."

"Then," said Willy, "it's no home to me."

"That's as you will, lad. You're fit to fend for yourself; but they're little use that doesn't stand by their own in trouble," said Lindsay quietly.

Eccles said nothing.

Both young men were sore and injured, and bitterly wounded in their pride, but he was the softer.

When the elder brother turned on his heel

and walked out of the cottage Eccles fidgeted about uncomfortably, going to the door once or twice, but always returning. Finally he kicked the fire into a blaze, and spoke to his father with hesitation.

"Will I straight things up a bit, father? You'll maybe want the bed up the room put to rights."

Lindsay looked up, and the eyes of the two men met.

"Ay, I'll be blithe o' your help, lad," he said.

That evening Ellen came home. She crawled up the lane with her father's support, finding every step an exhausting effort, and, luckily for herself, was still beyond feeling much except utter weakness and thankfulness for relief from pain.

She went to bed as soon as she arrived, but she could not sleep, for all through the long night the baby wailed.

The next day she dragged herself up, but only to sit before the fire with the child on her knee; she was too weak to be able for anything else, and too utterly dispirited. She was weighed down with shame; she would not meet her father's eyes nor answer him above her breath.

The baby was a poor, puny thing, with great eyes full of sorrow, and hands and feet like claws. It gave little sign of life beyond its feeble, fretful wail, and looked as if the troubles of the world in which it had appeared so inopportunely were too much for it. Mrs. Mawhinney's first words, when she came into the cottage in the afternoon, were, as usual, a prophecy of its immediate decease.

Ellen scarcely listened; her grandmother's

rasping voice was such a familiar sound in her ears.

She sat there, bent over her baby, and endured, while the monologue of reproof went on and on.

"It's a sorry heart I have this day because of you. You've brought trouble and shame on your own, and made an honest name a by-word. The Lord tells us that if we forsake Him He will turn and do us hurt and consume us, and it's His will that the innocent should suffer with the guilty. When them that should be Christians neglects the Lord's House the devil has an easy prey. Many's the night I've prayed on my knees for your conversion and the softening of your hard heart, and this is the end of it!"

Ellen sat, with the words scarcely penetrating to her brain. She was indeed a disgraced creature, at whom every one was privileged to cast a stone. She knew girls to whom the same thing had happened, and who had hardened not to care, and she wondered vaguely would she ever be like them.

She roused sharply to the consciousness that her grandmother was asking insistently for the name of the child's father.

"It's your duty to speak out the truth. It may be there are them could take the wean"— Ellen started—"or at the least help towards its keep. Who is the father?"

Ellen shook her head.

"There's been a talk of Archie Kennedy——"

"It's not him," said Ellen.

"There's no forgiveness for them that keeps a hard heart, and yours is hard. I am thankful your mother has been taken. Speak out, Ellen; who has brought you to shame?"

The girl was silent; she had heard the same thing so often, had had the same question asked so many times.

"At the least, he be to have spoke of marrying you, and maybe he would be willing to make an honest woman of you yet."

"There was no word of marriage," said Ellen steadily.

"And you're not ashamed to face me and say it, you bold-faced jade?"

"I *am* ashamed," said Ellen, very low.

Mrs. Mawhinney's voice was trembling with anger.

"If I was your father it's a good bating I'd give you. What has he said to you?"

"He's never said a word — he never spoke of it."

"He's just an omadhawn! It's useless wasting words on you or him; there's no shame in you!"

Mrs. Mawhinney's departure was always in hot anger, in that her words of wisdom seemed to have fallen on empty air.

Half way down the lane she met Lindsay coming back from his work, and was tempted to urge upon him a different method of treating his daughter, but his stern face checked her words. No one had dared to speak to him of the trouble that had come upon Ellen, and he had spoken to no one.

CHAPTER XV

For a long fortnight Mr. Duffin avoided the lake-shore—avoided anything that could remind him of Ellen, and tried to put away all thought of her. It was too late now, and useless to reproach himself with what might have been. So far he had escaped scot-free; Ellen must have kept the secret, and when she had kept it so long, why not for ever?

But he never went out without a dread of meeting the Lindsays in possession of the truth.

Surely, he told himself, in such a case his denial would be excusable, and would be believed. Confession would be of no use, and do harm to the parish, and even to the Church. And his sin was no great one.

He busied himself with the Unionist Club, the parish library, Orange meetings, and a service of song which was being got up in aid of the schools. There was always his rivalry with Mr. M'Cune to keep his interest awake.

And he tried to forget that the lake-shore was included in his parish.

But things could not go on like this always.

One day he was sent for to go and see old Mary Ann. She had come into the M'Faddens' cottage one day, and said she was "wore out and dwamish," and would be glad if they would let her rest.

Whereupon she had lain down in the little bed "up the room," and had never got up again.

There was nothing particular wrong with her; simply with the loss of her dogs her vitality seemed to have gone too.

She had not sent for Mr. Duffin herself, but some sound Churchman, having discovered in what dangerous company she was, had come to the rescue.

Mr. Duffin could not refuse, though he would have given worlds to be able to do so. All he could do was to wait till after dusk and hope for the best.

He found old Mary Ann in the little apartment, separated by a wooden partition from the kitchen, which was all the M'Faddens had by way of "a room." She was established in a very small child's bed, that stood on three legs with the assistance of a chair, and she had not discarded any of her many garments.

"It's all we can do for her, your reverence," Miss M'Fadden explained; "and it's little matter, for she'll soon be taken, poor old body. You'll likely be wanting to say a prayer or read a piece, so I'll lave you."

"If she is capable of understanding."

"Oh, I can understand rightly," said old Mary Ann fretfully, "and I suppose you may as well go on as usual now you're here; but I'm not overly fond of readin' and prayin'."

She listened to him more or less all the same, with her eyes following his movements, out of her mountain of head-covering.

Mr. Duffin was so nervous that he hardly knew what he was about. He was straining his ears all the time to catch every movement in the next room. He breathed a sigh of relief when he came out again to find only the M'Faddens.

"Old Mary ought to be in the workhouse," he said, "instead of burdening you."

"Indeed she ought," said Miss M'Fadden in her most happy-go-lucky voice; "but she's not willin' to go, and maybe, in her place, I wouldn't be either. It's not much she takes, poor old body, and there's plenty willin' to help. It was to that very room I tuk poor Ellen Lindsay not three weeks ago."

Mr. Duffin picked up his hat hastily and opened his mouth to say good-bye, but Miss M'Fadden was beforehand.

"It's a tarrable thing, such a decent, quiet wee girl. He must be an ill-doing rascal that brought the trouble upon them. The father will never hold up his head again."

"It's very sad," said Mr. Duffin.

"And to think of the rascal that done it getting off with nothin', and doubtless laughing in his sleeve. If I had my wull I'd hang the like of him like a dog; or, if I couldn't, at the laste I'd imprison him for nine months, with as good a flogging as ever he got at the end, and maybe he wouldn't be in such a hurry next time, the dirty, mane coward—and she no more than a wean."

It was the first time Mr. Duffin had heard the blame given to any one but Ellen herself. The other people who had spoken to him—and they had been many—had always, after a casual word of pity, pressed the weight of condemnation on the girl, and hardly seemed to remember that she was not alone in her guilt.

Some had raked up old stories against the Lindsay family, and asserted that there was "a bad drop" in them all; others had gone so far as to blacken what remained of poor Ellen's character, and hint that, for all they knew, this might not be the first time, and would certainly not be the last.

And Mr. Duffin had listened to the cruel words, and tried to convince himself that they might be true.

This other side of the question, which he had tried to ignore, disturbed him horribly. It delivered him helpless into the hands of Mrs. Mawhinney, who was on the watch for him by her door, and seized upon him resolutely.

"I have been looking out for your reverence. I have set my heart on a word with you, and if I hadn't heard you would be down this evening I would have made bold to go to the rectory."

Mr. Duffin was not grateful; at the same time he yielded to fate, but tried to stave off the evil moment by inquiries for the old husband, who was much as usual.

But after a few preliminary moments Mrs. Mawhinney spoke of Ellen.

"Your reverence has likely heard of our trouble. The Lord's hand has been heavy on us. I have never ceased prophesying to Ellen what would come of her running after sport and amusement to the neglect of her immortal soul. But it was then in her pride as it is now in her humiliation —naught I can say moves her hard heart. It's for that I made bold to stop your reverence. I have good behopes that if her minister spoke to her her heart might be changed."

Mr. Duffin, scarcely knowing what he was saying, began a confused suggestion of the possible effects of time; but Mrs. Mawhinney, after a pause for breath, broke through his words unheedingly—

"So I am about to ask your reverence if you would be so kind as to come up and spake to her. If you could get the man's name from her, maybe, if the Lord so allows, he could be brought to marry her."

In her eagerness the old woman laid a skinny claw upon Mr. Duffin's arm, to be sure that he was near in the darkness, and pushed her face so close to his that he could feel her breath.

He stood in great perturbation, frowning and muttering to himself and pulling at his moustache.

"I am afraid it would be useless."

"You won't refuse me? Ellen may be ill to move, but she could hardly withstand the authority of the Church," said the grandmother.

Mr. Duffin had excellent reasons for doubting Ellen's being impressed by the authority of the Church as vested in his person, but he could not say so.

Mrs. Mawhinney continued her speech, still putting forward her curious mixture of religious and worldly reasons for desiring his influence with Ellen. He only offered a passive resistance, and in the end he yielded.

Perhaps something was due to a desire to escape from the eerie grasp of the old woman's fingers in the darkness; but he yielded chiefly because of the absurd fear of a guilty man that if he did not his reason for refusing might be suspected.

But the situation seemed horribly grotesque.

As he groped his way up the lane, with Mrs. Mawhinney's hard-breathing and whining voice in his ears, he would have given worlds to escape. All sorts of horrible thoughts came to him. Once he started with the ridiculous idea that the Lindsays might have learned all, and that he was being led into a trap. When he had realised the absurdity of this he was consumed with another fear: if Ellen saw him before her now, would she still keep silence? And if she did not? And what possible thing could he say to her? If he was brought to her and forced to words of reproof, could she resist the temptation to say, "Thou art the man"?

Mrs. Mawhinney's voice droned on—

"The dure's just round to the left; keep clear o' the midden, sir, and mind the step."

Then, with her last words, she raised the latch of the door, and light from within came flooding out, dazzling Mr. Duffin's eyes for a moment.

Perhaps he had vaguely expected to find Ellen weeping and her father pacing the cottage in deepest despair; at any rate what he did see came upon him with a shock of surprise.

It was such a peaceful interior that it was hard to believe that the heaviest of troubles lay on the house. Ellen was sitting by the table, where she could get light from the candle, and was stitching busily—Mr. Duffin instinctively knew for whom. Her father sat a little farther back; he was smoking, and with his right foot he rocked a wooden cradle. There were rough, bright-coloured curtains pinned up over the windows, and the fire burnt cosily.

A flickering light from the candle fell on Ellen's pale face as she bent over her work.

The next moment she sprang to her feet with a sharp exclamation.

Mrs. Mawhinney advanced into the room, amiably introducing Mr. Duffin.

"It's his reverence," she said; "I asked him to come up and see if his words would have more weight than mine with Ellen."

She had never before made even such an indirect attack on her granddaughter before Lindsay, but Mr Duffin's presence encouraged her.

"I'm sure his reverence is aye welcome," said Lindsay stiffly.

"It's a late visit," said Mr. Duffin, trying to get the words carelessly from between his dry lips.

His eyes seemed drawn in spite of himself to Ellen and the cradle, from which came a faint intermittent cry.

Ellen's eyes were on the ground; she stood between her baby and him like a guard.

Lindsay got him a chair, and there was an awkward silence.

Mrs. Mawhinney, seeing the initiative left to her, was quite equal to it.

"His reverence is come to spake a word of seasonable reproof, and to say that you've a right to spake out, Ellen. He is about to tell you that it's your duty to fasten the sin where it belongs. Isn't that so, sir?"

Mr. Duffin sought for words to qualify the statement.

"I hardly feel I have a right——"

"And who would have a better right than the minister of God in her own parish? Maybe, if she gave his name, words from one who is an example to all the young of his parish might move the sinner to do all that's left in his power and marry her. Spake out, sir; she will hearken to you."

Mr. Duffin's words came in a stutter.

"What Mrs. Mawhinney says is doubtless right——"

Ellen raised her eyes very slowly and faced him. Such a look of reproach and scorn that he shivered before it.

Lindsay broke in while he tried to regain the thread of his words—

"I hope your reverence will take it as it's meant, but I should wish things let alone. The harm's done, and I'm overly willing to see to her and the child. I wouldn't have help from a rascal like thon if he went on his bended knees and prayed me to. So if your reverence would kindly talk of aught else."

But Ellen spoke in a strange voice.

"I would ask, does he want me to say the man's name?" she said.

Mrs. Mawhinney broke in gladly at this sign of relenting.

"Av coorse; isn't that what he's come for? And you'll be a wise girl——"

"He can spake himself, grandma," Ellen interrupted, with blazing eyes fixed on Mr. Duffin's face.

Mr. Duffin pulled his moustache, looking from right to left for escape.

"As Lindsay says, I fear I have no right to interfere," he said.

Mrs. Mawhinney was disgusted with her advocate's supineness.

It was her belief that a little more energy on his part would have won the victory, instead of which, after her one surprising outburst, Ellen fell back into her usual silent endurance.

Only once did she show any feeling again, and that was just before Mr. Duffin had succeeded in making his escape.

Her grandmother turned to her.

"Ellen," she said, "take up the wean. I'd like to show it to you, sir; you never saw such a misfortunate wee crowl in your life, and it just laments on without ceasing. It's not long for this world, and just as well, too."

But, with a swift movement, Ellen placed herself between her grandmother and the cradle. There was no mistaking her attitude, either by the two who did not understand, or by the one who did.

"She thinks shame," said the grandmother.

But it was not because she "thought shame" that Ellen stood between father and child with her young face set like a flint.

CHAPTER XVI

The long, monotonous days of winter crept on.

When the turf was in there was not much to do, and no work to be had. The weaving had fallen so low and was so hard to get that there were many idle looms and much dire poverty.

Lindsay was an old man, and could only work slowly; it took him nearly three weeks to finish a web and earn his eight shillings, and for the first time he and Ellen felt the pinch of real poverty.

The money which came from America was irregular—times were not too good there either; and Eccles, who was in regular work, had now his own home to provide for, while Willy had got drunk once too often, and been turned off and thrown for his livelihood upon odd jobs.

To Ellen this extra trouble seemed only part of the prolonged evil dream in which she was living. Somehow the days passed; she had the house to attend to and the baby; when her father was weaving she had the bobbins to wind for him, and there were always the goats and the hens. Except to go to the well she never crossed the threshold, and even that she put off till the early dusk of the evening, when there was no fear that she would have to face curious eyes. If people came into the cottage and she could not escape in time, she sat still and quiet in her corner, acutely self-conscious.

She never looked forward; probably had she done so she would have believed herself destined always to spend her days in the same way, with neither heart nor spirit to face the world again.

The baby was fretful and delicate, and held on to its life by a thread. Ellen was indifferent; she was too much of a child herself to care much about it, but Lindsay got used to it quickly, and then adored it.

Eccles and Eccles' wife often came in. Nancy Jane treated Ellen very scornfully—the more so, perhaps, that she was about to present her husband with an heir somewhat prematurely. But she was married, if a little late; and Ellen quite realised and accepted the vast distinction.

Willy stuck to his announced intention till he was thrown out of work, when he came home, having nowhere else to go. He consoled himself for thus deviating from his principles by scowling at Ellen, and never speaking to her unless it was absolutely necessary, and he was blind and deaf to the baby.

Ellen's most frequent visitor was her grandmother. Mrs. Mawhinney considered it her duty to come up constantly and give the girl long semi-religious lectures, interspersed freely with texts, chiefly from Isaiah and Revelation. She did her best to get Ellen to church, or to Plymouth Brethren or Methodist meetings, which were secretly more to her taste.

As an inducement she regaled her almost every afternoon with the story of three hard-hearted young men who had gone to a Methodist meeting in a tent one wet day. Their intention had been to mock and throw stones, but instead they had listened, been converted, and fallen face downward in the mud, crying out that they were saved. After which they had become thoroughly estimable members of society, and lived happily ever after. This tale was the only hopeful one in Mrs. Mawhinney's collection; the others all culminated in sudden death, "unsaved," or a lurid deathbed scene.

Ellen listened with her usual half attention. She was not saved, and she would go and burn in hell—no doubt of it; but with so many years of life before her she hardly felt as if she much cared. There was only one thing she did rouse herself to care about, and that caused her grandmother much displeasure; she insisted, and stuck firmly to it, that Mr. Duffin should not baptize her baby.

Her grandmother hotly opposed this queer fancy of Ellen's. Why should she go to another parish when a good and religious man, with no nonsensical High Church notions about him, was minister of her own? For her part she did not hold with Dr. Morton; she did not think it very decorus to see a minister of the gospel flying about the country on a cold iron wheel; and, what was more, they said he had to be watched pretty sharp in a baptism or he'd be making a cross on the water as well as on the child. And if Ellen would abide by her advice—which she never would—though maybe it would have been better for her if she had——

But Lindsay broke in, and said that Ellen should do as she liked.

The girl had sat silent, and to all appearance

unmoved, during the discussion; she drew a long sigh of relief when her father spoke.

Rather, almost rather, should her baby die unbaptized, and so burn in hell with her, than should Mr. Duffin touch it.

In all these long months he and she had never met; the desire for avoidance was equally sincere on both sides.

Mr. Duffin had almost managed to forget, but in forgetting he had hardened and become a worse man. He was morally more affected than Ellen. He had almost managed to put her out of his mind, and almost ceased to fear discovery; he could write his sermons without seeing a glaring application to himself spring up at every turn. When he succeeded in getting another parish he would be able to wipe this mistake entirely out of his life.

Till then, his occasional visits to the lake-shore to see old Mary Ann had a tendency to recall unpleasantly what he told himself was entirely past and done with.

Old Mary Ann was taking an unconscionable time to die. The M'Faddens would gladly have sent her to the workhouse now, but it was too late; she could not be moved. They were allowed a very few shillings to look after her, but Miss M'Fadden was worn out with day and night work all through the winter. Ellen Lindsay sometimes came in to help; Miss M'Fadden's kindly scrutiny hurt less than that of other people, and Ellen was a favourite of old Mary Ann's.

The old woman did not want to die; she fought hard for her life all through the winter, and pleaded passionately with the doctor for hope. All through the cold days of January and February it seemed as though she kept vitality in her shrivelled old body simply by her determination to live.

But when the March winds changed to the milder air of April, and everybody was busy putting in the crop, old Mary Ann all at once gave up the struggle.

CHAPTER XVII

"She's just a-waiting on, Miss Nelly."

The M'Faddens' cottage was full to overflowing. Behind Miss M'Fadden's stalwart, dishevelled figure Nelly Baring could catch a glimpse of men smoking over the fire, women sitting in cheerful groups, children who had come in pursuit of their mothers, and now hung curiously about the door of "the room."

A strange, ghastly attraction had brought all these people together to see an old woman die.

Nelly Baring drew back, and tried to subdue her clear voice to a decorous pitch.

"Poor old creature," she said, "I heard she was better yesterday, and I thought she might be able to take some soup."

"I am much beholden to you, Miss Nelly. But she's taken a scunner against everything, saving a drop of whisky the doctor allows her now and again. Ay, she was greatly set up by feeling so well yesterday, but I knew rightly it was nothing but a frolic before death. Won't you step inside, Miss Nelly?"

"No, thanks; there are so many there."

"A death still throws a stir. But you're as welcome as flowers in May, Miss Nelly, and maybe old Mary Ann would be fit to know you. If she does, she'll be quarely uplifted at seeing you. But she doesn't seem to know one, except"—(here Miss Miss M'Fadden dropped her voice to a whisper)—"except Ellen Lindsay."

Miss Baring paused irresolutely.

"Is she here? I don't want to see Ellen. I shouldn't know what to say to her. I am dreadfully disappointed about her."

"She's quarely failed," Miss M'Fadden whispered. "Have you never seen her since? And haven't you seen the lamenter?"

This was Miss M'Fadden's name for the baby, and needed some explanation.

Miss Baring allowed herself to be brought into the house somewhat unwillingly.

Most of the neighbours were congregated in "the room." Miss Baring, with a word to Barclay, was following her hostess when Mrs. Mawhinney, who was sitting in the shop window, stopped her to whisper an explanation of her presence.

"I never thought to see myself as long as I have been under a Catholic roof; but that poor, godless old body needs some one to see to her. It's tarrable for her to come to her latter end among Catholics. They are just watching to get the priest in to her, but if they do it will be across my body."

Mrs. Mawhinney looked exceedingly resolute. Nelly thought that Father Dymond, who was a small, delicate man, would have decidedly the worst of it in a struggle.

"Up the room" the laughing and talking had subsided into more decorous whispers on Miss Baring's entrance, and the groups drew a little apart.

Old Mary Ann lay very quietly, breathing

faintly and muttering to herself. Possibly the atmosphere of the tiny room, with all the windows not only shut but nailed down, no fireplace, and more than a dozen occupants, was no assistance to the drawing of difficult breath. But then, as Miss M'Fadden said, "it was quite time that she took a notion of dyin'."

They had expected her to die long ago. They had smoothed down her hands and tied a cloth round her withered jaws the evening before, and it had not seemed worth the trouble of removing it. But she was not dead; out of her small, shrunken face her eyes moved restlessly, following every speaker's words.

A stout matron, with a baby in her arms, related the deaths that had come under her personal observation, by way of making cheerful conversation.

"And he wasn't the man to spare expense. It would have done you good to see the beautiful lace and the flowers, and her hair all smoothed and curled as if for a wedden."

"It was the wasting sickness tuk her, if I'm not mistaken," said a friend, chiefly remarkable for a bright check shawl and very large, bare red feet, "and when that once takes a hoult there's naught to be done. Do you mind how the M'Guckins were taken—seven of them—as fine lads and lasses as you'd wish to see? But first the mother went, and then one after the other, as they came to grow up, they sickened and died."

Mrs. M'Gloughlan, the first speaker, hastened to put in her word:

"There was everything done for them. The father sent them to the salt water times and again, even with the last ones, when he knew he was wasting his money. They say he's quare and lonesome now he's none but himself."

"I am afraid that's the way with our Jenny," said another woman, pointing out a thin, stooped girl leaning against the bed. "I was in two minds about marrying her father, and I would better have left it alone. He hardly ever was fit for a day's turn till he died. And now there's Jenny—what will she ever do for me?—and she'll hardly be here come Holiday."

Everybody looked at Jenny, who flushed with a gratified sense of importance. If her mother's struggle for life, with a dying husband and delicate children, had hardened her into such words, she had nursed them, and nursed Jenny now, with passionate devotion. The girl had always known herself to be doomed, and took a curious pride in it.

A man, who had taken his pipe out of his mouth in deference to Miss Baring, now joined in—

"Do you mind Hughie Thompson's old mother? She died in the House, and as soon as he heard it he ups and takes a coffin and a car and had her well buried too, and no stint about it."

"The only dacent thing he did was to take her out," said Mrs. M'Gloughlan, shaking her head. "They all like to be buried at home. There was Patrick Kennedy; them that he was with in America set great store by him, and offered to see to him the best, and have him buried in their own grave when he was giv' up by the doctor. But no, he must get home somehow; and home he got, and as soon as he saw the lake-shore he tuk to his bed quite content, and the breath left him before morning."

"One likes to be with one's own at the last,"

said somebody else. "Sure, if her niece," indicating the shrivelled form on the bed with her thumb, "had any dacency, she'd bury her at the laste."

"She'll not need to be beholden to her," said Miss M'Fadden; "sure, his honour gave me what will bury her comfortable."

There was something like a flash of intelligence and satisfaction in old Mary Ann's eyes.

"It's lonesome to be left like that," said the check-shawled neighbour; "there's where them that has childer has the best of it."

"I've childer enough, if they look to me," said Mrs. M'Gloughlan. "Annie there is coming on ten or eleven, I don't rightly mind which, and there are six behind her. I would sooner have had boys, but there's them says that if you get daughters well placed they'll maybe do as much for you."

"And likely enough more. Look at Hughie Thompson letting his old mother go to the House, and he a warm man. That old body looks dwamish, Jane; she'd be the better of a drop of whisky to wet her lips."

"It's little use troubling," said Miss M'Fadden; "indeed it's near wore out I am minding her. It's time the poor old body tuk a notion of dyin'. I am not fit to stand another night of it."

Miss Baring had found the conversation very ghastly; most ghastly of all it seemed to her now that old Mary Ann's eyes, as she turned them from one to another, were pleading for a little more time."

Ellen Lindsay rose from a seat in the background, raised the old woman's head, and gave her a spoonful of whisky.

It seemed to revive her, and she spoke for the first time, in a thin thread of a voice—

"Is it you, darlint? Heaven's blessings on you for your goodness. It's a fine swaddy you are. I'm quarely mended. It's dancin' I'll be at your wedden before long."

Ellen, with a crimson face and lips trembling piteously, tried to disengage herself.

"Dancin' at your wedden," old Mary Ann repeated, while Ellen was conscious that a smile went round the cottage.

"Don't you see Miss Nelly?" said Miss M'Fadden.

The old woman was propped up in bed to help her breathing; the white linen round her face made it look particularly shrunken and yellow; she had the appearance of a mummy only half revivified.

Nelly found it an effort not to shrink when the skinny hand made a feeble effort to reach hers.

"Heth, dear! is that Miss Nelly? Did you hear that they'd took away the dogs and drownded the puppies? Maybe if you would spake to his honour or her ladyship I would get back Charlie, against I'm fit to be going about? Sorra one o' them was equal to Charlie."

"It's tarrable to see one so near her end thinking of the like of that," said Mrs. M'Gloughlan, shaking her head.

The faint voice went on—

"Come forward then, dear, till I see you proper. I'm quarely mended. Would you like me to lilt you a song?"

"Just lie still, dear, and don't be wastin' your breath," said Miss M'Fadden sensibly, but old Mary Ann would not heed her.

With Nelly's hand in hers she began a long, long song, chiefly unintelligible, about a young woman who went to a fair, and had various strange and not very edifying adventures. There was a breathless silence in the room; nobody had ever heard the old woman sing before, except to her dogs when she believed herself to be alone with them.

On and on the weak voice quavered, and no one knew exactly when it ceased. Nelly took a moment or two to realise the silence, then she softly drew away her hand and left the room with relief.

Miss M'Fadden had taken Ellen's baby from little Annie M'Gloughlan. Ellen laid old Mary back on the bed, amidst a murmur of horrified comment.

"If she was singing hymns it would be more fitting her than them godless songs."

"Miss Nelly might have said a word of prayer."

"I don't know that Miss Nelly's overly good at the prayin'," said Mrs. M'Gloughlan; "but she's pleasant-spoken, and that plain and free it might be you or me. She's maybe right to leave the prayin' to his reverence, and if the sough's true she'll never be far pairted from him."

Ellen raised her head.

Miss M'Fadden gave an exclamation of denial.

"Heth, not likely! Sure, he's good enough, I dare say; but it's not the like of him, rared on potatoes and buttermilk, that will even himself to Miss Nelly. Are you away, Mrs. M'Gloughlan? I jaloused you would wait and help me to lay her out. It won't be long. From the look of her I'm thinking she's set about dyin' in real arnest."

"I'll be over later. I have to go home to get his tea," said Mrs. M'Gloughlan, alluding to her husband.

Ellen felt the house stifle her. She left her baby with Miss M'Fadden, and crept out alone, making her way up the gorse-covered hill by the lake, which went by the name of the "Whinny Hill."

She lay down on the grass, putting her fingers in her ears to try and shut out the sound of old Mary Ann's rattling breath. The echo of it seemed to follow her through the clear evening air.

Down below, on the road, a couple of horses were going home from the plough; a boy was riding one, sitting sideways with dangling legs and whistling shrilly.

A boat crossed the lake with sails fully set to catch the faint breeze; another was close to the shore, and Ellen could hear the splash of the oars and the voices of the fishermen. A flock of peewits that they had disturbed rose, circling round uncertainly with soft cries.

Suddenly the sound of the six o'clock bell from the rectory came clearly across the bog.

Ellen buried her face in her arms and tried hard not to hear; the air seemed full of noise this evening, and she wanted to think.

The faint sweet smell of the gorse came to her; new golden blossoms were budding everywhere amidst last year's grey, faded branches. In a month or two the hill would be one mass of yellow.

Just in sight some very small children, who

had been dropping potatoes all day, but had not exhausted their energy, were playing games in a ring, with a gleam of red frocks among the whin-bushes. Last year Ellen had played with them scores of times; now she felt so old, so very old; she knew she would never play with them again.

She had been working in the fields all day, leaving her baby in charge of little Annie M'Gloughlan, and with her return to work, to warmth, and to plenty of food, her strength was coming back, and bringing with it the sharpest suffering. She had not recognised in the least that it was in a great measure her physical weakness which had enabled her to bear the hopelessness of her life with dreary resignation. Now all the youth and strength and love of joy in her was rebelling.

Mr. Duffin could and would marry—perhaps Miss Nelly.

Ellen would have accepted it as the natural course of events, and without resentment, had it not been for his broken promise. That, she told herself, she never would forgive him.

The children on the hill played on, and their voices came to her in an old rhyme which she had sung almost every day of her school life :—

> "Georgy-porgy, pudding and pie,
> Kissed the girls and made them cry;
> When the boys came out to play,
> Georgy-porgy ran away."

Ellen could not have told any more than the children the sense of the words, or what connection they had with the game they belonged to, but the sound of them distracted her thoughts.

She was a miserable girl. Miss Nelly had looked at her scornful-like, and every one thought little of her, and she could not bear it.

It would be aye the same. When a girl had once lost her character nothing she could do was of any use. There was no hope for her; she had thought she might be like some girls she knew, and mind it less after the first, but instead it had grown worse to bear—never had it been so bad as this day.

There was this left to her—she could drown herself. She would be away from them all then, and perhaps they would think less hard of her; and her father would bring up the baby, and teach it to be a good girl, and find his comfort in it.

Mr. Duffin would be sorry; he would know then that she did not take things light, and he would not be able to forget her.

She drew herself slowly to her feet, and went down the hill with lingering steps.

The fowls had all come out to revel in a newly ploughed field at the foot. As she passed through, the turkey-cock opened his wings with a "tchuck" of anger at being disturbed. He was the only one who paid any attention to her whatsoever, the rest were much too deeply engaged in their own affairs. A compact party of ducks were foraging about at a rapid, cheerful trot, with an insufferable air of self-satisfaction. They were a great deal too busy to get out of Ellen's way, and she had to wait while they swaggered across the path.

She sat down by the side of a deep, black bog-hole. Willy had said only that morning that a man could be easily drowned there. What would he say when he found his sister's dead body?

She sat on the edge with her bare feet dangling. When they touched the bank the soft turf crumbled beneath them.

She would be dead—dead as old Mary Ann would soon be—stiff and cold.

She saw herself laid out on her bed at home, with the neighbours round, and Willy perhaps sorrowing for his harshness. They would dress her out in white, and bring her flowers as she lay in her coffin.

Ellen was revelling in a luxury of misery of which she was honestly quite unaware.

The children's voices came more faintly across the field :—

> "Now, young couple, we wish you joy,
> Every year a girl and a boy."

It seemed like a mockery. Ellen shuddered at the thought of herself in the cold water, while they played on :—

> "Now, young couple, come kiss together."

She moved her place till her foot touched the soft bottom, which began to give way under it.

Probably no one would ever find her; she would sink down and be lost, and so best. Her father would be sorry at first, but the baby would comfort him.

She began to slip a little.

A clear burst of laughter came to her from the children.

The cold bog water rose silently round her feet. Suddenly she gave a cry of terror and clutched wildly at the turf on each side of her. For just one moment the struggle was a doubtful one. She fought eagerly for her life, dragging herself up by the rushes and heather. It was all over very quickly. When she found herself panting and breathless, but alive, she sank down on the heather and burst into bitter sobbing.

She could not do it. She realised her cowardice with a sharp pang of despair. There was no escape for her this way—she must live.

Two nights later she was roused from her sleep by shouts and outbursts of tipsy merriment. "The boys" were going home from old Mary Ann's wake.

It might have been from hers; a half-inch nearer the edge, a little more courage, and she too had been lying in her coffin.

She clasped the baby closely and warmly to her, and wondered if she was sorry.

CHAPTER XVIII

The summer had come. The bog glowed with colour, and the "Whinny Hill" was one mass of yellow. For more than half a mile out the lake had dried up, and the marshy grass was dotted with red and white cattle.

Eccles and his wife had walked out, as they often did of a Sunday afternoon, and had found Lindsay and Ellen in the field.

Lindsay had carried out the baby and laid her on the grass beside him; he was smoking meditatively, but every now and then he stooped to pat her cheek or take her in his arms and toss her high till she laughed. She was a puny creature still, with a brow of care and great sad eyes, but with Lindsay even Ellen was growing to take a second place.

Ellen sat in shelter of the hedge with her lap full of marigolds that she had gathered in the long grass, not yet cut for hay.

She did not take much notice of Eccles and his wife, but she moved a little to give Nancy Jane a place beside her.

"It's faired up well since yesterday," said Eccles as a greeting.

"It looks like a good Twelfth," said his father.

All remarks upon the weather for the last fortnight were understood to have reference to the great "12th" of July.

"It'll be three years since we had it dry," said Eccles, "and it *be* to be dry this time, for there's no shelter within near a mile of the field. There'll be fourteen Lodges, I was countin'. Three from Sloughlan, forby two from beyont the lake——"

He went on reckoning up on his fingers with much satisfaction.

"And great speeches, I'm thinking."

"That indeed. There'll be Dr. Morton and the Colonel, and two speakers from Dublin, forby them from all round. Mr. Duffin is to speak."

"And I'll hould he'll say something worth listening to. He's still one that's not feared to say what's in his mind."

"It'll be the best Twelfth we've ever had," said Eccles enthusiastically.

"I am in two minds about going," said Nancy Jane. "If the baby was weaned, and I could lave it with Ellen, or if they met near hand—but there's little pleasure in four miles, carrying a heavy wean, and four back, so maybe I'd better bide at home."

Ellen sat absolutely silent with an expressionless face. The last Twelfth had been the most intense delight. There had been dancing and singing and twelve bands; she had had a new dress, and for the first time in her life people had begun to treat her as a woman. Archie Kennedy had put himself out all day to get a word with her, and Ellen had enjoyed with all her heart her first taste of power.

Eccles looked at his wife and laughed.

"Hark till her!" he said; "as if she had any more mind to stay at home than myself! If that's the way of it, Nancy Jane, it's unbenownst to me why you're getting a new dress—to set at home in, maybe!"

This effort of wit was received with much amusement.

"Maybe I'll go after all," said Nancy Jane with fine indifference; "and I was thinking, if I do, likely you'd give me the loan of your umbrella, Ellen. It's better nor mine, and my dress is that light it would be drookit in a minute."

"You can have it," said Ellen ungraciously.

It was hard—hard. She could have borne it better if they had even seemed to think it possible she might want to go. But now she must always be at home—she would never again have any change or pleasure, and no one thought of her or cared.

It would be always the same. Nancy Jane could be agreeable enough when she wanted anything, but it never occurred to her that Ellen was still a living girl and not an old woman or a machine.

She got up abruptly, and her sister-in-law followed her into the house to secure her umbrella.

Lindsay looked after them, and smoked in silence for a few minutes.

"Eccles," he said, "I'm onaisy about the wean. She's just breaking her heart. You see, her trouble's aye before her here, and her grandmother is still casting it up to her, and that carnaptious and ill to please. I've been coming round to think she would be best away."

"But you couldn't do wanting her."

"I was coming to that. I have been wondering if it would suit you and Nancy Jane to come and live out here. There'd be no rent, and I'd pay my board if so be as she would mind the little one "—he touched the baby—" and maybe, as she has her own, it would be little more trouble."

Eccles looked uncomfortable.

"I'd be glad if you could see your way, lad. You won't lose by it. And the wee thing's that ould-fashioned it 'ud be little trouble. Ellen's never had a chanst. Maybe this would never have come if I'd let her go to Philadelphy when they sent for her. But if they are willin' to see to her now, I'll let her go, and get the ticket somehow, and ask them for nothing."

Eccles said he would think of it. He was taken by surprise, and not sure how Nancy Jane would receive the proposition; to know this was all-important, as hers was decidedly the stronger will.

When she appeared in triumph with the umbrella they both went home.

Ellen did not come to say good-bye. She was miserable, and hot with rebellion against fate. Was she to be condemned to stay at home next day, when not a soul would be left in the country but Catholics?—when every one would be happy, and Mr. Duffin would be speaking on a platform?

She was to spend the long lonely day as best she might, and in the evening be ready to welcome the none too steady steps of her father and Willy.

She would not stand it—she would not. She would go and enjoy herself with the best of them, and let those who chose say a word—she did not care!

CHAPTER XIX

THE field was gay with flags and bright dresses and orange scarves, and noisy with the sounds of many drums.

A gorgeous arch of orange lilies, with an effigy in coloured shavings of King William on a prancing steed hanging from the middle, marked the entrance to the festive scene and the skill and taste of the Ballymagra Lodges.

The Ballyturbet Orangemen had only just arrived, after a hard morning of it. They had been marching in and out of Ballyturbet since daylight, and had gone two miles out of their way to meet the Sloughan Lodges; after which it had been necessary to honour the rectory and the manse, as well as the Barings and the Lawsons, with ceremonious marches past, which had all taken time and energy.

The Lodge masters, in their scarlet and gilt robes, had had the best of it; their gaunt white horses, marvelling at having exchanged their plough for a bunch of orange lilies between their drooping ears, had carried them steadily along in dignified fashion.

The hardest work had fallen upon the flag-bearers and the drummers; they looked exhausted and exceedingly damp, though they had thrown off their coats and made sundry pauses to refresh themselves. Willy Lindsay was already doubtful where he ended and his drum began, and had had difficulties in steering clear of the sides of the orange arch.

Eccles, decorated with a coloured scarf and a sword, and in charge of Nancy Jane and the baby, was so far commendably sober.

At the end of the procession came a crowd of women and children in their best clothes; for the most part they, too, looked hot and draggled, and were eager to make their way to the stalls which lined the field, or to find a corner where they could sit down and enjoy the provisions they had brought with them.

At present both men and women kept to themselves, and there was little mingling of sexes; it would be different later on.

Ellen had joined herself defiantly to a party from the lake. She laughed and talked loudly, with a flushed face, and tried to believe she was enjoying herself.

"I declare if that isn't Ellen Lindsay!" said one woman to another. "Did you ever see such impidence? Not a bit of shame in her!"

"To my eye she looks as if she had had a sup," the other assented.

The words did not reach Ellen, but she felt them—she felt them in the looks and manner of all her neighbours.

But what did she care? What did it matter to her?

When the speeches began she went with the rest to stand below the wooden platform in the middle of the field. She looked very young and pretty; several people on the platform noticed her flushed, defiant face, with its frame of yellow hair.

When Mr. Duffin rose to speak, received by Ballyturbet cheers, she moved her position a little till she could see him better, and watched him with hard, curious eyes.

He did not mince matters in his speech, and his words were thoroughly to the taste of his hearers. He spoke of their ancestors' blood which had been shed by Catholics, and hinted at a possible necessity for more bloodshed in the future. If so, who so ready as the brave boys he beheld before him? Cries of "To hell with the Pope!" and cheers.

"On whom should Ireland depend to strike a necessary blow in her defence but on her Orangemen? He was sure there was not one here this day who was not ready to fight to the last drop of his life's blood to save his country from the ruin, the utter destruction of Home Rule!"

An outburst of cheering interrupted him.

This was what they wanted—this was what they had come to hear.

"Father," said a boy who was standing near the platform, "do you mind that girl's face?"

"I can't say as I do."

"Don't you mind that wet evening she come so often to know if the man was there to marry her?" said the boy. He had opened the door many times to Ellen, while his father had only seen her once.

"Three cheers for the Reverend Mr. Duffin!" cried a voice in the crowd.

The red-haired boy started.

"And it was him she asked for!" he said.

"Hould your whisht and don't talk foolishness," said the registrar.

The crowd round the platform began to break up.

Ellen followed Mrs. M'Gloughlan, but that worthy woman was tired, and soon found a comfortable bank, on which she sat down abruptly, with a generous exhibition of white-stockinged legs. A selection of youthful daughters established themselves in her skirts, and several old cronies, eager for a gossip, completed the circle. They did not want Ellen.

She went farther on, and joined herself to a group of girls who had gone to Miss Nelly's class with her a year ago. Then she had been the most popular among them, and the centre of all fun, and her society had been in great demand. Now they were not unkind, and spoke to her civilly enough.

But in the past year she had fallen out of them; she did not know their jokes and stories, and her place had been filled. This girl, who was nervously bold, and yet crimsoned when they spoke to her—who had neither the spirits nor the self-confidence to be amusing—was like a ghost of the Ellen Lindsay they had known, and missed, and gossiped about.

In those days she had been the leader; now the plainest and stupidest felt herself to be condescending to her.

Two older girls, in some sort cousins of the Lindsays, stopped and spoke to her in a friendly way, but their young men came up and she was forgotten.

One or two men spoke to her, among them Archie Kennedy, who passed her with a careless word and a perfunctory attempt to kiss her.

But though he, at least, recognised her as the prettiest girl there, and the one who attracted him most, he knew he would be laughed at if he had anything to say to a girl who had "come to trouble."

The Barings drove up to the field in the afternoon, and once Ellen found herself face to face with Miss Baring. Nelly turned away her head, nodding in a friendly way to the other girls in the group, and exchanging a whisper with one of the Lawsons. Ellen knew as well as if she had heard the words that they were an expression of disgust with her shamelessness in being there.

She moved away, her eyes smarting with tears, which she kept back with all her strength.

She did not like to be seen by herself, and tried to look as if she belonged first to one party and then to another. She drew towards them, remaining at a little distance, which might have been accidental, so as not to be in the way. Nobody was unkind; they simply did not think about her, and had all their own friends and amusements. But she was very glad when it was time to turn homewards, and a sleepy, cross little M'Gloughlan was thankfully confided to her.

Her father she had scarcely seen all day; now he went on among the first, while she followed a group of matrons who got themselves over the ground with much deliberation.

The procession was decidedly less orderly in its return; there were a good many stragglers missing, and every now and then some one dropped out of the ranks, either irresistibly attracted by a public-house, or in consequence of having been so attracted earlier in the day.

Willy Lindsay still had his drum, and was dancing along the road, transformed by drink and excitement into a dangerous maniac. His face was damp and crimson; his hair stood on end; his shirt was torn and dirty, and lay open at the throat. Even his drum had suffered; one side was battered in, the other was stained and bloody. He beat it furiously, calling in a hoarse voice for the Catholics to come on, if they dared face an honest Protestant boy, and qualifying them with many adjectives. As they wisely declined to be beguiled, he suddenly turned upon the nearest flag-bearer, who was quite inoffensive and marvellously sober, and struck him in the face, accusing him of being a Catholic in disguise.

A general row was only averted by the starting of a hopeful rumour that the genuine article was to be found a little farther on, armed with sticks and staves. But this ended in disappointment.

Eccles was being helped along, and at the same time restrained, by Nancy Jane; he, too, was "fighting drunk," and being armed with a sword, and in the midst of a group similarly armed, he was more dangerous.

After the main body a string of interlaced couples straggled in twos, and occasionally threes, when some lucky youth was fortunate enough to secure a lady on either side.

There was a general straightening up among the soberer individuals when the Barings drove through them, followed by Mr. Duffin in his dog-cart.

Mr. Duffin was elated, and pleased with the success of his speech; he was thinking of it as he drove past, and did not even see Ellen, though she had to move out of the way to let him pass, and his wheels sent a cloud of dust in her face.

Neither did he notice that in one or two places the men of the procession drew together with whispers and strange looks as he drove by.

CHAPTER XX.

Nobody ever knew exactly how the rumour first started. Probably when the registrar, by the merest chance, exchanged what he knew of Ellen Lindsay's story for what a couple of Ballyturbet men could tell him. At any rate, within a week from the Twelfth, a very unpleasant whisper had spread everywhere about Ballyturbet.

People began to remember that Mr. Duffin had singled out Ellen as a favourite, and then had suddenly and inexplicably dropped her. One or two neighbours by the lake recalled, or imagined, having seen them together.

One thing was found to fit in with another, and Mr. Duffin was followed by unpleasant looks, which had not yet developed into words.

He went on his way rejoicing, and quite unconscious of any trouble in the air.

He was quite sufficiently employed in quarreling to the death with Mr. M'Cune over a piano which had been bought by the Temperance Society of joint Church and Presbyterians. The society had now split into two sections under their respective clergymen, and neither would yield or sell their half of the piano. They could not possibly agree to share it still, as in all the year they had fixed upon the same evening on which to desire it—one for a concert, and the other for a Service of Song.

Mr. Duffin and Mr. M'Cune exchanged several letters daily, and had the daily excitement of trying to be first in securing the piano for a practice.

Consequently Mr. Duffin had no time to think of anything else, and remained quite unconscious of the cloud which was ready to burst over his head.

The rumour reached the Lindsays last. When Eccles heard what his neighbours were saying he went to Willy by instinct, not being given to take the initiative, and Willy, as usual, was the one to act. He said very little at first, but it was remarked that for one whole week he was absolutely sober. At the end he had apparently satisfied himself and made up his mind.

All summer through a goodly contingent of Ballyturbet men went every Wednesday and Saturday evening to play football in a field near the village.

The next Saturday, just as the game was over and the players were putting on their coats, Willy Lindsay strolled slowly into the middle of them, and took up his position against one of the goal-posts.

"Boys," he said, "will you bide a bit? I've something to say to you."

There was a pause. Willy Lindsay was not given to much speech when he was sober, and he was undoubtedly sober now.

They surrounded him expectantly as he stood.

Willy spoke in a rough, deliberate voice, and without hesitation.

"You all know of the misfortune to my sister. I'm not telling you a new story in speaking of our shame."

He paused; a murmur went through the group, and they drew closer together.

"And of these last weeks you've all heard a father given to her child. Now, boys, I'm not saying a girl shouldn't mind herself, or isn't to blame. But what I'm wanting to ask you is this"—Willy's voice grew louder, and his face filled with an excitement which was reflected on the faces round him—"Is all the sufferin' and shame to fall on the one ill fitted to bear it, and is the other to go free? Is the other to have never a punishment—for what I've *proved*, mind you—just because he's one of the quality and a disgrace to the Church?"

There was an outburst of exclamations and oaths.

Willy cleared his throat and went on with increasing excitement.

"To my mind, boys, it's a d——d sight worse in a gentleman uplifting and moidering a poor girl with his words and ways, that she's not used to, than in the like of us. I've spoke to Sir William Lawson and Mr. Baring, and they won't believe it. If the law won't help, it's for us to help ourselves. Are you willin' to send your sisters and daughters to Sabbath-school to be taught by one who, as like as not, is thinkin' to lead them wrong? Are you willin' to sit every Sabbath under a man who has been the ruin of one poor girl at the laste?"

He was interrupted by a general shout of "No! no!" supported by a good deal of strong language. Several men said they'd be d——d if they would, and one went so far as to assert that he'd go to the Presbyterians first, which was understood to be almost a stronger way of putting it.

"It's for you to say if you'll help us, boys, or if it's none of your business. As for me, may I lose all chanst of the Lord's mercy, may I be struck down dead at your feet and rot in hell for iver, if I'm not revenged on that black-hearted divil!"

Willy had raised his hand in denunciation; he let it fall and wiped his hot forehead, while a hoarse, excited outburst of curses broke out.

His words had had their effect: the storm had burst.

CHAPTER XXI

"It's all done for no other reason than to oppose me, Miss Nelly, and it's always the way with the Presbyterians."

"That's exactly what Mr. M'Cune says of you," said Nelly. It was Sunday morning, and she anp Mr. Duffin had arrived in Sunday-school very much before any one else, so she was kindly employing the interval in endeavouring to teach him how to govern his parish.

"Probably Mr. M'Cune does say so," said Mr. Duffin with dignity; "but allow me to explain to you the full truth of the matter, and how it happens that the piano——"

"Please don't tell me," said Nelly, "or you won't be in a Christian frame of mind for your class. And you know, whoever is right, it seems to me a great fuss about nothing."

Mr. Duffin was divided between his desire to stand well with the Barings and his irritation at her boldness.

"You will perhaps allow me to observe," he said solemnly, "that you speak in this manner because you scarcely understand. This matter concerns the proper position of the Church in the parish, and surely, Miss Nelly, you will admit that there is nothing so important?"

"I must say I'm fond of peace," said Nelly,

who would have fought to the death for her own way.

"But it is hardly right," said Mr. Duffin, "for the sake of peace in this world to give up working for heaven."

Nelly laughed.

"Do you really think that they care in heaven whether you have your concert on Monday or Tuesday?" she said.

Mr. Duffin never knew whether to be shocked or not when he was with Nelly Baring.

He took a middle course now, and said, with a slight accent of reproof—

"It is the principle concerned, my dear Miss Nelly. It would be easy and pleasant to give in for peace in this world, but heaven is more important—that we must look forward to as our great object."

"I don't know that I'm so very keen about going to your heaven," said Miss Baring, shrugging her shoulders; "there'll be nobody there except a few Ulster Protestants, and it's sure to be dull."

She tried Mr. Duffin hard. He paused, and said, with a constrained smile, that it was very pleasant for Miss Baring to have such cheerful spirits.

But she was quite unabashed.

"And in the meantime," she said, "before we get to heaven, how are we to spend this morning upon earth? Shall I ask you questions on the two last chapters of Joshua, or will you take the chance of finding me a docile pupil?"

"Yes, it's very strange," said Mr. Duffin; "there isn't a sign of any one."

It was strange undoubtedly; it was several

minutes past ten, and not a child had come to fill the empty forms. Presently the schoolmistress and monitress arrived, rather breathless with a sense of lateness.

Nelly sat on a table and yawned openly for about a quarter of an hour after she had exhausted her conversation; then she went home, very much perplexed, and related her experiences to her family.

When he heard it Mr. Baring seemed disturbed. He had by no means forgotten his interview with Willy Lindsay the day before, and he did not feel so sure as he had assumed to be that the rumour was unfounded.

"I suppose I'd better go to church," he said; "there's the chance of a row, and Lawson is so hot."

"Oh, then you're in the mystery," said Nelly pertly.

"Get your prayer-book, my good girl, and mind your own business," said her father, from whom she had inherited her sharp tongue, with several other peculiarities.

All was quiet as they went up the church—the only sign of anything unusual was that walk; the bell was not ringing, and that the group of men round the church door was large and purposeful.

As the Barings came up one of them advanced, touching his hat.

"I beg pardon, your honour; there will be no service this morning," he said.

Mr. Baring threw a rapid glance over the small crowd; he saw it was chiefly composed of young men, dressed in their ordinary Sunday attire, but one and all provided with stout sticks. The few women and children that were there had drawn a little apart.

Mr. Baring spoke as if all was as usual.

"Eh?—no service?" he said. "What brings you here, then?"

"We're waitin' on his reverence," said the man grimly.

He had scarcely finished speaking before Mr. Duffin entered the churchyard, and a murmur and movement went through the crowd.

Mr. Duffin made a momentary pause in surprise, and then came on towards them.

He had been very much puzzled by the sudden boycotting of the Sunday-school, and the nearest parents, to whom he had gone, had had but feeble excuses for the absence of their children.

Now he saw that there was something seriously wrong, but no idea of the truth entered his head. He had grown to feel so secure in his months of impunity.

"There'll be no service the day," said the man who had spoken to Mr. Baring.

Mr. Duffin turned on him sharply.

"What's the meaning of this? Why is the bell not ringing at this hour?"

"The bell's not ringing because the sexton can't get in to ring it. We've been at the trouble of nailing up the dure here, and the vestry dure the same. There'll be no service the day."

"Nor as long as you're in the parish, ye black-hearted divil!" said Willy Lindsay, suddenly springing forward.

The repression of the crowd failed at his words; there was a quick outburst of rage, and here and there a hand was raised threateningly, or closed in a tighter grasp round a stick.

Mr. Duffin grew suddenly white. All at once he understood what it meant.

Mr. Baring came forward.

"Hold back, boys; what's all this about? Behave like rational beings, and open the church door. You must choose a proper time for anything you have to say."

"If they don't open it at once I'll get the police and have it burst with a crowbar!" said Mr. Duffin passionately.

"You'd better not," said M'Gloughlan. "Lave him to us, your honour, and we'll tache him what we have to say."

"But he'll never cross this dure again, unless it's feet foremost," said Willy, raising his stick significantly.

Mr. Baring faced them gravely.

"You're not setting about this right, boys," he said. "If you have some accusation to make against Mr. Duffin—an accusation which I have no doubt he can easily disprove—this is neither the time nor the place for it. Lindsay, you are an old man and a sensible one——"

"Your honour," said Lindsay, "I'm loath to go again you, and I don't say if I was doin' it I'd maybe choose just this way. But the boys have taken it upon themselves, and I'm told they went to you and Sir William first. Lave it to us, sir. That false-hearted divil isn't fit to live. He's ruined and desthroyed my child, and that's what I put to him to deny if he dar!"

"He says right," said M'Gloughlan; "it's aisy for your honour, but his daughter's as much to him as Miss Nelly, there, is to you; and he's been so wrought that he would thank God had she been buried a year ago in this churchyard.

Your honour, what each man here says to himself is this—'If it hadn't been his daughter it might have been mine.' We see to them as well as we can, but it isn't aisy, and many and many a mother just breaks her heart over the fear. And what can we do again a *gentleman* like thon?"

Mr. Duffin's face was like chalk. Mr. Baring saw it when he looked at him.

"I can understand all you say, believing this, boys, but every man should have a fair chance. I have no doubt that Mr. Duffin can easily convince you that you are wronging him."

"Such an accusation scarcely deserves a reply," said Mr. Duffin hoarsely.

"But it needs one," said Mr. Baring.

"Of course—of course—this is all a painful mistake. You have been deceived and misled——"

"Not another lie out of you!" said Archie Kennedy, Methodist and Sunday-school teacher, ending with a burst of opprobrious names.

Mr. Baring felt it was time to end the scene.

"You're the strongest to-day, boys," he said, "think what we may of your action. I hope you will disperse quietly, and I promise you that the fullest inquiry shall be made. Mr. Duffin will certainly desire it. I only wish you had set about it better."

"Maybe if it was your house and child he'd brought to shame, you'd hardly be troublin' about politeness," said M'Gloughlan.

Mr. Duffin muttered something about a crowbar, but Mr. Baring shook his head and drew him down the drive. He saw the men looked dangerous, and was doubtful if his presence would restrain them long.

He walked up to the rectory with Mr. Duffin, and heard his denial repeated. Mr. Duffin agreed that inquiry—the fullest inquiry—must be courted. It was most unpleasant and painful, he said, and Mr. Baring assented dryly.

He could not bring himself to believe the denial.

CHAPTER XXII

Mr Duffin was a very miserable man. The blow had fallen so suddenly, and after he had grown to such a sense of security.

He considered it, tramping up and down his room, as was his habit when much disturbed, frowning and pulling at his moustache while he muttered to himself.

Betty had spread a cloth over one half the table, to save herself the trouble of removing his books from the other, and had laid out his dinner —a chop and a couple of potatoes, all rapidly getting cold. But he was not in the humour to eat.

Had his absolute denial been wise? There had not been time to think, and he had spoken on impulse. He had been most unfairly taken at an advantage.

But it was too late to trouble about that now; he must stand by what he had said, and face it out—and he would.

Once he had been almost ready to let all go for Ellen's sake. But it was too late to think of that now; Ellen could never be anything to him, and he had ceased to wish it; the thought of her aroused nothing but a sense of irritation and resentment.

It must be, he thought, through her that discovery had come, threatening him with absolute ruin—absolute ruin at least from a social point of view. Mr. Duffin doubted if otherwise he could be made to suffer much.

What steps would be taken? He did not know. But he felt himself an ill-used man, and exceptionally unfortunate in that he had not removed to another parish in time.

He had several days to think things over, and very unpleasant days they were. If he ventured out he met cold looks and avoidance from every one, sometimes scowls and muttered threats, which he was obliged to ignore. If he remained indoors he was overwhelmed with Betty's effusive sympathy and championship of his wrongs.

Every day rubbed away a little more of the carefully cultivated suavity of his manner. When Dr. Morton came to see him towards the end of the week, he faced him, metaphorically showing his teeth like a dog driven to desperation.

Dr. Morton, who was in the habit of taking men as he found them, without much perception of character, was amazed at the change in his manner, which he found utterly inexplicable. Mr. Duffin would have liked to be civil and careless, but he could not hide his soreness, nor strike the medium between somewhat servile politeness and rudeness.

Dr. Morton was very much embarrassed, and found his mission very difficult. Had he believed in the other's innocence it would have been easy enough, and no one would have been so hot and eager as Dr. Morton to champion his cause. But confirmation of the first report had come in from every side; one after another people had begun to remember and put things together, and there seemed little room left for doubt.

Dr. Morton's frank face was very red, and his words did not come so easily as usual. He stood, leaning against the mantelshelf, unconsciously playing with a vase of withered flowers which Betty had once gathered and arranged in a fit of lavishness, and then apparently considered an ornament for all time.

"Of course this is very unpleasant," he said.

"Exceedingly unpleasant—for me," said Mr. Duffin.

"For you and for us all," said Dr. Morton, taking up the vase and looking at it sternly. "Of course we believe your denial—you understand that—and the Bishop feels that the whole thing must be kept as quiet as possible; but still he considers an inquiry will be absolutely necessary —for your sake."

Dr. Morton was embarrassed between his own private conviction and the necessity of treating a man as innocent till he was proved guilty.

"The rumour is utterly false," said Mr. Duffin, "but unless it is disproved it means ruin to me. So neither for the sake of obliging the Bishop nor saving the Church from gossip can I be expected to extinguish myself."

"Of course," said Dr. Morton, who was pulling the head off one flower after another, in absolute unconsciousness of what he was doing, "but you will scarcely find the parish comfortable in the future——"

"I shall not resign, under any circumstances. I am having a crowbar made to break open the church door next Sunday; if necessary I shall fight it, and if the Bishop turns me out it will be for him to compensate me."

"You must, of course, do as you think best," said Dr. Morton, "but it is always a mistake to raise a scandal."

But in his heart he sympathised with Mr. Duffin's intention of fighting it.

"It's the one decent thing about the man," he said hotly to Mr. Baring afterwards, "that he has some pluck."

Mr. Baring shook his head.

"Bluster, but not pluck. You'll see he won't do it. What will be done to him?"

Dr. Morton fumed to himself.

"He'll have to come before a diocesan court, I suppose—most unpleasant."

"And what then?"

"What then—what then? Why, then the scoundrel ought to be hung! I don't mean that. Of course there's no absolute proof, and we are bound to believe the best."

"But I suppose he won't be hung?" Mr. Baring persisted.

"No; not exactly."

"And what will be done?"

"I hardly know—I hardly know what the Bishop has power to do. He might suspend him and put in a *locum tenens* for six months or a year. But I'm afraid he can't turn him out of the parish."

"Good God! do you mean a clergyman may do what he likes and can't be turned out or punished like a man in any other profession?"

"Oh, not exactly that," said Dr. Morton vaguely, because it was exactly what he did mean.

"And one can't help realising," said Mr. Baring, "that the Bishop is hardly the man——"

Dr. Morton stiffened and grew clerical at once.

"The Bishop is placed in a very difficult position," he said.

"Damn it all!" said Mr. Baring, in an outburst of anger. "I wish with all my heart I had not been such a fool as to interfere between him and the beating he so richly deserves!"

CHAPTER XXIII

It was autumn again.

Once more the Barings and the Lawsons were in the garden, playing tennis and eating apples. The year had brought little or no change either to them or to Ballyturbet.

Mr. Baring, as he sat by his study window, looked a man with whom the world had gone very easily. In truth, he had had the same troubles as his neighbours, over tenants and a vanishing income, but he was blest with a glorious capacity for fuming over things one minute and totally forgetting them the next.

This afternoon he pished and pshawed over his letters in a very ruffled frame of mind.

Nelly came round and tapped at the glass.

"Father, the Lindsays are at the door asking for you," she said.

"Very well, very well," said Mr. Baring impatiently. Then, as Nelly turned away, he threw up the window and called to her, after a helpless fashion in which he sometimes appealed to his womenkind.

"Nelly, what the devil am I to say to the Lindsays? Do you know what they've done about Mr. Duffin? Here's a letter about him. It seems there was some question at first of suspending him for a year, but in the end they struck a bargain with him. He wouldn't yield an inch till the Bishop promised him a recommendatory letter, and a hundred and fifty a year till he gets another parish of equal value. And they gave in."

"Father!" said Nelly, "why, they're *rewarding* him! It can't be true."

"It's true enough. Fifty pounds is to come out of the new incumbent's pocket, and a hundred out of a fund for deserving clergy; and I haven't a doubt the Bishop will write him a glowing letter. That's clerical justice!"

They looked at each other.

"And what am I to say to the Lindsays? I urged them to leave it to the law—like a fool," Mr. Baring ended hotly, his indignation getting the better of him.

"Say!" cried Nelly vehemently. "Say it's the most wicked injustice and crying shame you ever heard of! What else *can* you say?"

"That's so like a woman!" said Mr. Baring pettishly. "Of course I can't say anything of the sort."

He sent for the Lindsays, after a doubt about the advisability of seeing them at the hall door, and he certainly made an effort to put the best complexion he could on the thing.

Willy advanced, cap in hand, and was spokesman as usual.

"I am sorry for disturbin' your honour," he said, "but we were thinkin' you might have heard about Mr. Duffin?"

"Well, yes, I have. Take a seat, Lindsay. I may say I have heard."

"They're sayin' in the town that, far from the

Bishop punishing him, he's made him a present of money and written praising him up. But I don't doubt it's a mistake. The like of us often take up things wrong."

"It's not exactly like that," said Mr. Baring, playing with a paper-knife. "You see, there is not much the Bishop could do; it was necessary to come to some agreement. He couldn't oblige Mr. Duffin to leave the parish——"

"Then it's true, sir? It's true they're giving him one hundred and fifty pounds every year for what he's done? They proved he done it, didn't they, sir?"

"Yes, I suppose so."

"And do you think they're doin' right?" said Willy.

The question was too much for Mr. Baring. He suddenly flamed up—

"No, I do not! I think it's an abominable injustice. But there is nothing to be done. I am very sorry for you."

"Maybe," said Willy gravely, "I'll find a way to settle with him yet."

There was nothing more to be said. After a pause they both went away gravely and quietly.

"So he's got off clear?" said Eccles, with an oath.

"Maybe he has, and maybe he hasn't," said Willy. "See here, Eccles, will you stand to me?"

"'Deed and doubles I will."

"And there's plenty more will. I've not kep' my eyes shut nor my tongue tied, and I happen to know that dirty brute has taken away naught that belongs to him. I've made it my business to know. And as that's so, he'll hardly do without coming down to see to things, once at the laste."

"Do you think it?" said Eccles.

"Ay; there's a lash of things to see to. He'll come, and—we'll be ready for him."

The two men exchanged a long look of comprehension.

CHAPTER XXIV

THE short November evening had closed in. The only light, as Mr. Duffin drove through the bog, was from the lamps of his car, or where, at long intervals in the sky, one or two stars were making a faint appearance.

He had been at the rectory all day, arriving early, and working hard to get everything done. He had had a last interview with Betty, and arranged what things were to be packed, and what was to be sold by auction; he had sent off his horse to a dealer, and made arrangements for the disposal of his dog-cart. Finally, he had gone round the house, the yard, and the garden, and could feel he had neglected nothing.

Now he was free; that chapter of his life was closed for ever.

He had thought it best to arrive early and go back late, by way of avoiding any unpleasant meetings, and he had hired the car from a man who was not one of his parishioners, and whom he had never known.

Now, when he had left Ballyturbet behind him for ever, when he could feel the breeze across the bogs blowing in his face and see the glimmer of light from the Lindsays' cottage for the last time, he breathed a long sigh of relief.

His troubles were over, and he was full of

hope. He had a fresh start before him, somewhere—perhaps in England—where nobody had ever heard of Ballyturbet; he was one of the exceptionally lucky in life who are given another chance. And he could afford to wait till the chance was a good one. There was no hurry; he would look about him and consider, and this time he would not fail.

Fortune was on his side, and who could tell how high he might rise in the future?

In the dark Mr. Duffin smiled to himself with entire satisfaction.

The road through the bog was narrow and not too safe, and they were driving slowly and cautiously.

Mr. Duffin from his seat watched the cottage lights grow smaller and dimmer with a dreamy sense of contentment.

"Stop—damn you, stop!"

The shout broke through the darkness with startling suddenness, interrupting the peaceful flow of Mr. Duffin's thoughts of the future.

The driver drew up abruptly, so abruptly that if they had not been going at the slowest of trots the horse would scarcely have kept his feet.

They came to a full stop in the darkness.

"What is it? What are we stopping for?" said Mr. Duffin, annoyed at being roughly roused out of his dream.

He put out his hand towards the driver, and found, with a shock of surprise, that the man had jumped from his seat. Somebody grasped the horse's head so roughly that it drew back, nearly sending the car off the road, and a stone struck Mr. Duffin on the forehead.

He put up his hand in a bewildered way to

wipe off the blood he felt slowly trickling down his cheek. What had happened? What was going to happen?

"Is anything wrong?" he said in a sharp voice of alarm.

He got no answer; there had so far been no further words about it at all. But suddenly a dozen strong arms gripped him and drew him from his seat.

He was thoroughly awake to his danger now. He struggled desperately, and he was a strong man, but his efforts were useless against so many.

"What is it? What are you going to do, boys?" he said hoarsely.

"Settle with you for the girl you've ruined."

Somebody said the words, and to Mr. Duffin they came like a shout through the silence, and repeated themselves again and again in his head: "Settle with you for the girl you've ruined—settle with you for girl you've ruined."

A cold terror fell upon him; the sweat gathered on his forehead, and he shook from head to foot with mortal fear.

"My God! are you going to murder me?"

Then in a moment he was beneath a rain of blows. They fell upon his back, his shoulders, his head; the men were half drunken, and did not measure their strokes.

He struggled hard at first, striking out into the darkness, fighting silently, with thick, gasping breaths, for his life. After a time he fell forward on his knees.

He uttered no cry. There was no sound at all, except the heavy breathing of the men and the thud of their blows.

All at once he slipped through their hands and fell on his face in the road.

The blows ceased. There was a pause, while the men stood in the darkness with idle hands, suddenly sobered.

"He's kilt entoirely," said Archie Kennedy, meaning that his beating had been a severe one.

"I'm afeard it's worse than that," said Eccles hoarsely.

Willy broke the silence that followed.

"Give us a light," he said. "Where's the lantern, Archie?"

He took it, and knelt down beside the fallen man, sending the light full upon his ghastly, blood-stained face. He tore open the shirt and laid his hand on his heart, during a few minutes' breathless expectation.

Then he rose to his feet, and the lantern showed a dozen white faces.

It had all happened so quickly. A few minutes before the man at their feet had been a living, breathing man, full of hope and satisfaction with life; now he lay there no longer at their mercy.

One of the group broke the silence in a voice of horror.

"God knows we've gone too far," he said; "we didn't mean this!"

Archie Kennedy burst into sobs; he was nothing but a boy, and he was frightened and only half sober.

"If we had a docthor there might be a chanst yet," said Eccles Lindsay.

His brother stopped his irresolute movement.

"You'll go for no docthor, you fool. The man's dead; there's no docthor in the world could mend a broken skull. He's got what he desarved, and no more, and we've to look to ourselves. Andy Murdoch, take your car and be off, and mind you know none of us the night. Archie, quit makin' a woman of yourself, and take a hoult of the body round the oxter. We'll lave him in a grave where it'll be long enough before they find him."

"What are you going to do?"

"I am goin' to let the bog swaller him, as it's done many a betther man," said Willy grimly.

A shudder went through the group; to some this seemed the most cruel thing of all, but none of them liked to speak. They were dismayed by the darkness and the suddenness of it all, and obeyed Willy by instinct.

Unwillingly, but without putting their opposition into words or action, they took up the body and carried it off the road, down a path which led into the bog. They went slowly and carefully, picking their steps by the help of the lantern. Choose their path as they might, the feet of the men, carrying their heavy burden, sank above their ankles in the soft peat.

"Easy now," said Willy; "we'll lave him here."

They paused; at their feet the lantern shone on a dark, still pool of water.

"Let him go," said Willy.

Eccles gave a quick cry: "I can't! I can't! It's a wicked thing."

Willy turned on him.

"You fool! You know what it manes to us? It's him or us. Let the body slip, Archie, and mind your own fut"

They lowered him slowly. Willy, who was foremost, stepped too near, and felt the ice-cold water creeping round his ankle. He started back with an exclamation of horror, and, his support being removed, the body fell into the water with a sudden splash.

Wet drops flew into the men's faces; young Kennedy, shivering and sobbing, wiped his cheek feverishly again and again.

In the light of the lantern the circles in the water grew gradually less distinct; while they stood silently it closed, dark and quiet as ever.

" He's there till the Judgment Day," said Willy. " God forgive him."

" And God forgive us!" said Archie Kennedy under his breath.

THE END

A SELF-DENYING ORDINANCE

By M. HAMILTON

In One Volume, price 6s.

The Athenæum.—'The characters are exceptionally distinct, the movement is brisk, and the dialogue is natural and convincing.'

The Pall Mall Gazette.—'Joanna Conway is on distinctly new lines, and it has given us pleasure to follow her spicy, attractive personality through all the phases of her carefully, finely-depicted evolution.'

The National Observer.—'A remarkably life-like picture of English society. The author is a keen observer. The writing is above the average.'

The Daily Chronicle.—'An excellent novel. Joanna Conway is one of the most attractive figures in recent fiction. It is no small tribute to the author's skill that this simple country girl, without beauty or accomplishments, is from first to last so winning a personality. The book is full of excellent observation.'

Black and White.—'Some pleasant hours may be passed in following the fortunes of Joanna, the charming heroine of M. Hamilton's *A Self-Denying Ordinance*. The book is well written, and holds the attention from start to finish. The characters are true to life.'

The Methodist Times.—'The story retains its interest throughout. It contains some vividly-drawn delineations of character.'

Woman.—'Contains the finest, surest, subtlest character drawing that England has had from a new writer for years and years past.'

Public Opinion.—'A well written and fascinating novel. It is a clever sketch of life in its different phases. . . . "Every personage strikes one as being richly endowed with individuality."'

The Manchester Courier.—'A decided success. There are such women as Joanna Conway in the world, though, unfortunately, not so many as are required; but there are few writers of the present day who can do justice to such a character, so poetical, and yet so practical. . . . There is humour in the book: the scene is chiefly in Ireland, and who can truly write of Ireland without humour? but the greatest charm is in the wonderful tenderness, in the womanly chivalry which renders so true the title of a self-denying ordinance.'

LONDON: WILLIAM HEINEMANN, 21 BEDFORD STREET, W.C.

THE YEARS THAT THE LOCUST HATH EATEN

By ANNIE E. HOLDSWORTH

In One Volume, price 6s.

The Literary World.—'The novel is marked by great strength, which is always under subjection to the author's gift of restraint, so that we are made to feel the intensity all the more. Pathos and humour (in the true sense) go together through these chapters; and for such qualities as earnestness, insight, moral courage, and thoughtfulness, *The Years that the Locust hath Eaten* tands out prominently among noteworthy books of the time.'

The Daily News.—'Bears out to the full the promise given by *Joanna Traill, Spinster*. The author has a genuine sense of humour and an eye for character, and if she bids us weep at the tragedy of life and death, she makes us smile by her pleasant handling of human foible and eccentricities.'

The Standard.—'A worthy successor to *Joanna Traill, Spinster*. It is quite as powerful. It has insight and sympathy and pathos, humour, and some shrewd understanding of human nature scattered up and down its pages. Moreover, there is beauty in the story and idealism. . . . Told with a humour, a grace, a simplicity, that ought to give the story a long reign. . . . The charm of the book is undeniable; it is one that only a clever woman, full of the best instincts of her sex, could have written.'

The Review of Reviews.—'It has all the charm and simplicity of treatment which gave its predecessor (*Joanna Traill, Spinster*) its vogue.'

The Pall Mall Gazette.—'The book should not be missed by a fastidious novel-reader.'

The Court Journal.—'The moral of the book is excellent; the style strong and bold.'

The Scotsman.—'The story is well told, and a vein of humour serves to bring the pathos into higher relief.'

The Manchester Guardian.—'It is sincere and conscientious, and it shows appreciation of the value of reticence.'

The Manchester Courier.—'The book is full of delicate touches of characterisation, and is written with considerable sense of style.'

The Glasgow Herald.—'Worked out with great skill and success. . . . The story is powerfully told.'

The Liverpool Mercury.—'The story is told with sympathy and pathos, and the concluding chapters are touching in the extreme.'

The Birmingham Gazette.—'A sad story beautifully written, containing pure thoughts and abundant food for reflection upon the misery which exists in the world at the present day. The tale is particularly pathetic, but it is true in character. It will be read with interest.'

The Leeds Mercury.—'Full of powerful situations.'

LONDON: WILLIAM HEINEMANN, 21 BEDFORD STREET, W.C.

HERBERT VANLENNERT

By C. F. KEARY

In One Volume, price 6s.

The National Observer.—'Clever characterisation, natural dialogue, moral sanity, and keen observation and knowledge of the world. . . . The minor characters are as diverse as they are numerous, and there is not a lay figure in the book.'

The Daily News.—'*Herbert Vanlennert* is good throughout. The analysis of the hero's character is excellent. The story is crowded with minor characters, all clearly individualised and seen in nice relation to their surroundings. There is much power of observation, much knowledge of life and art displayed throughout.'

The Pall Mall Gazette.—'A piece of life and a work of art. . . . Mr. Keary's men and women are solid all through. He is as honest in his presentation of life as Mr. Gissing, but he is more pointed and wittier; he is less witty than Mr. Meredith, but he is more responsible. . . . Mr. Keary's work stands out as a very brilliant piece of honest, knowledgable, wise artistry. We say it deliberately, that there are very few novels of our time that bear so unmistakably the grip of the master-hand as *Herbert Vanlennert*.'

The St. James's Gazette.—'A novel like this helps us at once to understand, to judge, and to enjoy life; and that is to say that he has written a novel of the kind that only the great novelists write. From time to time there comes a new novel marked by a kind and degree of excellence that compels praise of an emphatic kind. There need be no hesitation about deciding that *Herbert Vanlennert* is such a book.'

The Review of Reviews.—'In *Herbert Vanlennert* indeed is a whole little world of living people—friends and acquaintances whom it is not easy to forget.'

The Sketch.—'Full of cleverness and a legitimate realism. Of two of the most strongly marked and skilfully drawn characters, one is Maynard, the artist of genius; the other, a striking contrast to Maynard, is Bernard, who passes a serene existence in the study of metaphysics. Very charming and interesting are Mr. Keary's bright and vivid descriptions of English country life and scenery in Derbyshire.'

St. Paul's.—'The book contains much clever writing, and is in many respects a strong one.'

Black and White.—'There is abundance of skilfully drawn characters and brilliantly sketched incidents, which, once read, cannot be forgotten.'

The Scotsman.—'Mr. Keary, even when he is treading on delicate ground, writes with circumspection and cleverness.'

The Bradford Observer.—'It is a fine piece of art, and should touch its readers to fine issues.'

The Manchester Courier.—'The book is most interesting, and embodies a great deal of careful work, besides some very plain speaking.'

LONDON: WILLIAM HEINEMANN, 21 BEDFORD STREET, W.C.

MISS GRACE OF ALL SOULS'

By W. E. TIREBUCK

In One Volume, price 6s.

The Times.—'Since Mrs. Gaskell wrote her *Mary Barton* we have seen no more interesting novel on the condition of the working classes. Mr. Tirebuck is thoroughly master of his subject. ... A vivid and impressive narrative of the great coal strike of a couple of years ago.'

The Literary World.—'Every reader anxious to hear of a work that is full of brains and vigour may unhesitatingly enter *Miss Grace of All Souls*' upon his list of books worthy to be perused. ... Mr. Tirebuck, not content with providing "Grace" for our admiration, has made another claim upon our love by presenting us to Nance Ockleshaw. For her sake alone *Miss Grace of All Souls*' should be read, and we hope that the novel will make its way into many a home, there to be considered with all the care that is due to it.'

The World.—'The most remarkable contribution made by fiction to the history of the working classes since *Mary Barton*, and it has a wider range and import of deeper gravity. It appeals directly to the thoughtful among readers, those who care to learn, on the object-lesson plan, the facts and aspects of life among the multitudes, with whom they are brought into actual contact. The girl who is its central figure is an original and very attractive character.'

The Daily Chronicle.—'An uncommonly well-told story, interesting from first to last. Mr. Tirebuck has drawn a truly delightful character in the miner's wife; indeed, the whole family might well have been sketched straight from the life. It is difficult to make a work of fiction at once instructive and entertaining, but Mr. Tirebuck has done it in *Miss Grace of All Souls*'.'

The Pall Mall Gazette.—'An admirable piece of work. Here is realism in its proper proportions: the rude, harsh, Methody life of the northern miner engraved in all its essentials. Mr. Tirebuck manages to illustrate the conditions of miners' lives for us with complete fidelity. Not a touch of the humour, the pathos, the tragedy, the grime, the sin, and the ideals is lacking. ... Mr. Tirebuck has done his work to perfection. The story is not a moral tract, but a work of art of great significance.'

The British Weekly.—'Mr. Tirebuck is a practised and powerful novelist, and in this story he has taken us right inside the heart of the poor. His description of the collier's wife is wonderful work.'

The Manchester Guardian.—'As a picture of working men and women, instinct as it is with knowledge, sympathy, passion, and conviction, we have seldom, if ever, read anything so good.'

The Manchester Courier.—'The character of Miss Grace reminds the reader of the heroine of Charles Kingsley's *Westward Ho*.'

LONDON: WILLIAM HEINEMANN, 21 BEDFORD STREET, W.C.

The Pioneer Series

The Athenæum.—"If this Series keeps up to the present high level of interest, novel readers will have fresh cause for gratitude to Mr. Heinemann."

The Daily Telegraph.—"Mr. Heinemann's genial nursery of up-to-date romance.'

The Observer.—"The smart 'Pioneer Series.'"

The Manchester Courier.—"The 'Pioneer Series' promises to be as original as many other of Mr. Heinemann's ventures.

Black and White.—"The brilliant 'Pioneer Series.'"

The Liverpool Mercury.—"Each succeeding issue of the 'Pioneer Series' has a character of its own and a special attractiveness."

Price 3s. net, uniformly bound in cloth; or, in ornamental paper wrappers, 2s. 6d. net each volume.

The Pioneer Series

VOL. I.

Joanna Traill, Spinster

By ANNIE E. HOLDSWORTH

The Observer.—"Every word tells that it is the work of a true woman who has thought deeply and lovingly on a most painful subject. . . . The picture is a beautiful one, which it would be well for many women to ponder over. . . . In her claims for wider sympathy, a higher understanding of right and wrong, and her noble picture of woman helping woman, the authoress has done a good work."

The Methodist Times.—"This is an exceedingly fine work of fiction."

The Gentlewoman.—"Will rank among the prominent books of the year."

The Guardian.—"Shows marked power of drawing character, and character of no commonplace kind. . . . A very clever and very suggestive book."

The Saturday Review.—"'Joanna Traill, Spinster,' is so grave in subject, so passionate and earnest in treatment, and so absolutely right in morals, that one might suppose the series intended to lead into high regions of pure reason."

The Publisher's Circular.—"A remarkably clever piece of work. . . . The 'Pioneer Series' starts with an initial volume as remarkable in its way as that which initiated the 'Pseudonym Library.'"

The Morning Leader.—"Mr. William Heinemann could hardly have done better than start his 'Pioneer Series' with the noble and courageous story of Annie E. Holdsworth. . . . A novel charged with real human characters subtly drawn."

The Sun.—"Alive with character and movement. . . . In point of construction and completeness, it is quite a model for the series it inaugurates, and it will fare far below its deserts if it does not attract considerable attention."

The Pall Mall Gazette.—"The interesting story is powerfully told. Boas is drawn with keen fidelity; the touch of humour is supplied in the characters and proceedings of Joanna's married sisters, who are skilfully worked into the closing tragedy of her noble and selfless life."

St. Paul's.—"It is a problem book, and the problem is courageous, and one of the newest in fiction."

The Daily Telegraph.—"The character of the spinster is admirably drawn throughout, with a sympathy and insight which reveal no small measure of artistic gift. Miss Holdsworth evidently has both power and pathos."

The Pioneer Series

VOL. II.

George Mandeville's Husband

By C. E. RAIMOND

The Athenæum.—"The chief merit of the book lies in the portrait of the husband. . . . There is very great dramatic propriety in many of the little touches which indicate his nature, and contrast it with his wife's . . . and a very just effect is conveyed by the gradual metamorphosis of his Bohemian and unconventional joyousness. A most excellent and powerful piece of work."

The Pall Mall Gazette.—"This novel is a good novel, and it is to be sincerely hoped will not occasion a storm of blasts and counter-blasts, as we fear it may. . . . Its author is a very able writer, and a keen, if rather brutal, satirist."

The Literary World.—"Mr. Heinemann has certainly 'struck oil' in 'George Mandeville's Husband.' . . . This story of paternal love will stick in the memory of every one who reads it."

The World.—"Mingled humour, pathos, just protest, and unanswerable, straightforward, strong common-sense, in a style refreshingly vivid, realistic, and effective. . . . The story of the artist and his little daughter is painfully pathetic, and a fine test of the severe simplicity of the author's style."

The Spectator.—"George Mandeville herself is an even more effective picture than George Mandeville's husband; and the third figure in the little group described in it—their child Rosina—is the most delicate and exquisite study of the three. . . . Mr. Raimond is undoubtedly an artist of great power. . . . He certainly understands women's distinctive graciousness and ungraciousness, as few women of the advanced type appear to understand it."

The Pall Mall Budget.—"Clever, biting, and irresistible."

The Observer.—"Charmingly written, light of touch, and interesting from first to last, with some delightfully humorous bits, and here and there a phrase full of pathos."

The Daily News.—"That the author can write with grace and pathos is shown in the presentation of Rosina. The relations between the father and child are very tenderly described. The book is written in nervous and easy English. It is exceedingly clever."

The Guardian.—"A novel of rare concentration, combined with powerful delineation of character, . . . and told in the most admirable English."

The Glasgow Herald.—"It is a really clever and careful bit of work, and both in conception and execution is very different from the ordinary average novel. . . . The 'Pioneer Series' ought to be a success if succeeding volumes have anything of the same high quality as 'George Mandeville's Husband.'"

The Pioneer Series

VOL. III.

The Wings of Icarus

By LAURENCE ALMA TADEMA

The Athenæum.—"On the whole, Miss Alma Tadema has succeeded in the difficult task of titling a story in letters. . . . The book is remarkable for the vividness with which the feelings of a woman in love are realised. Many writers have shown, as it were, from outside the most charming women in love, but that is not the same thing as entering into those feelings almost personally, as Miss Alma Tadema has done."

The Daily Chronicle.—"Taken simply on its merits, 'The Wings of Icarus' is a very creditable performance. It is pleasantly and unaffectedly written, and it tells, or rather indicates, a really tragic little story."

The Globe.—"The exhibition of the inner soul of Emilia is of such absorbing interest, her emotions are delineated with so much force, yet with so much delicacy, that the mind of the reader is wholly taken possession of, and Emilia's woeful love-tale has all the fascination of a classical tragedy, . . . unquestionable literary charm, a rare refinement, and a fund of poetic suggestion."

The Daily Telegraph.—"In our opinion, the intrinsic merits of this brilliant booklet justify the belief that in time to come the illustrious name of Alma Tadema will earn as high honour in connection with written romance as that which it has hitherto acquired by association with painted presentments. . . . An intensely pathetic tale of passionate love and ineffable self-sacrifice. . . . Nothing has been more impressively told in the pages of modern fiction than the *dénouement* of this sad but deeply fascinating story."

The Sketch.—"The working out of the story is novel enough, . . . 'The Wings of Icarus' is a book of promise. There is a large amount of fine work in it. In the interpretation of delicate shades of sentiment Miss Alma Tadema is already skilled."

The Daily News.—"The character of the heroine is very cleverly portrayed. . . . Constance is a suggestive sketch; the feebleness of her nature is redeemed by the pathos of her fate. Miss Tadema writes eloquently."

The Pall Mall Budget.—"Miss Alma Tadema has written with fidelity to a type, and a good deal of genuine feeling."

The Liverpool Mercury.—"The story of a woman's heart-break, powerfully written, deeply interesting, but also very sad."

The Manchester Courier.—"As a revelation of the character of a woman's passionate and unbalanced nature it is exceedingly powerful."

The Pioneer Series

VOL. IV.

The Green Carnation

By ROBERT HICHENS

Punch, in the "Blue Gardenia (a colourable imitation)."—"Archie, I am writing a book. . . . It will be called 'The Blue Gardenia.' The title is one of the unemployed; it has nothing to do with the story. . . . I shall not lack the art of personal allusion. If my characters go out into the village, and see the village clergyman, I shall make him the Archbishop of Canterbury. People like it. They say it's rude, but they read the book and repeat the rudeness."

The Times.—"Amusing enough."

The Observer.—"It is likely to rouse a great deal of interest and excitement, being modern of the moderns, daringly personal often, and from the first page to the last bristling with well-pointed spears, sparkling with epigram, and glittering with wit, sarcasm, and delicious cynicism. It is intensely entertaining and up-to-date. . . . The temptation to quote is almost irresistible; but where there is such a superabundance of good things it is difficult to choose. . . . The book is a classic of its kind, and its witty scorn at the insipidities of a cult run to seed is admirable."

The Daily Telegraph.—"One of the most brilliant expositions of latter-day humour that has been brought to the public cognisance for many a day."

The World.—"Brimful of good things, and exceedingly clever. It is much more original, really, than its title implies. . . . The character-sketches are admirable."

The Globe.—"'The Green Carnation' is unquestionably an entertaining book. . . . The author of this latest social satire has done his spiriting gently. . . . Mr. Esmé Amarinth is doubtless intended for a portrait, not for a caricature. . . . One of the most consistently amusing that has been given to the public for some time."

The Sketch.—"There is plenty of clever satire in it."

The Illustrated London News.—"The general public will like 'The Green Carnation,' . . . because it is full of fun and humour, and has no page whereat you may not laugh loudly. . . . The student of literature will be interested in it, because it marks a further development in the form of satire invented by Peacock in 'Crotchet Castle,' and adopted by Mr. Mallock in the 'New Republic.' . . . The writer of 'The Green Carnation' is . . . quite as witty as either of his two models, and has all Peacock's talent for buffoon description of incident, and Mr. Mallock's pretty power of giving you a whole man or woman in a little flash of words. His style has grace. He is a nicely equipped satirist."

The Pioneer Series

VOL. V.

An Altar of Earth

By THYMOL MONK

The Speaker.—"It is not merely clever, but pathetic and natural; and although the author has not been able to resist the temptation to introduce that question of the Seventh Commandment, which is apparently the one question that has any interest for the New Woman, she judiciously gives to it an interest that is merely hypothetical."

The Gentlewoman.—"'An Altar of Earth' belongs to the impressionist-cum-realistic method that finds such popular favour for the moment. Of its kind the book is more than a fair example, and apart from the excellent construction of plot is marked by many happy terms of expression. . . . A neatness of thought, and an aptness for suggested characterisation, give the tragic story great strength."

The Saturday Review.—"The latest volume of Mr. Heinemann's 'Pioneer Series' maintains to some extent that tradition of originality, and of that quality, which we have agreed to call 'modern,' that previous volumes in this series have led us to expect. The book . . . is a book of much promise. It is exceedingly well written; and . . . there is pathos and genuine dramatic power."

The Sunday Times.—"'An Altar of Earth' is a slight, pretty, and well-written story, with a rather curious culminating incident. . . . There is a summery, pine-tree air about the little story which is very pleasant; the dialogue is bright, and Daphne is delicately and cleverly drawn, in spite of the shadow of death that hangs over her during the whole story. She is much the cheeriest person in the book. . . . This volume of the clever series should also be very popular."

The Sun.—"There are touches in the book that remind one of 'An African Farm,' and the descriptions of Surrey scenery are charmingly fresh and true. Like its predecessors, the book is decidedly unconventional."

The Observer.—"It is a pathetic little story."

The Dundee Advertiser.—"Powerful in its unwonted pathos, the story is not the least noteworthy in a remarkable series. . . . It is of unique merit, and distinguished by an odd beauty of indefinable fascination."

The Glasgow Herald.—"The book is distinctly clever and readable. . . . On the whole, she has written a striking and powerful book."

The Pioneer Series

VOL. VI.

A Street in Suburbia

By EDWIN W. PUGH

The Globe.—"The first sketch, 'The Courtship of Jack Cotter,' indicates a sense of humour which Mr. Pugh develops later on; but more to the credit of this little book than its attempts to amuse are the cleanness and the wholesomeness of its simple ethics, and its avoidance of unsavoury details. . . . This 'Pioneer' writes well, has an eye for dramatic effect, and has observed local humours with fruitful appreciation."

The Sketch.—"By humour and pathos of a healthy kind, and not a little literary skill, Mr. Pugh has given some very vivid pictures of poor London life. There is one scene, in the chapter called 'A Small-talk Exchange,' describing the desperate venture of a child with a farthing at its disposal into a sweet lottery, which, in its way, for shrewdness and veracity, it would be hard to beat. And there are other scenes and stories, too, with the breath of life in them. 'A Street in Suburbia' is the best of the 'Pioneer Series,' not forgetting 'George Mandeville's Husband.'"

The Daily Chronicle.—"These short sketches of low London life show observation and the assiduous use of a note-book. . . . Mr. Pugh has more sympathy with, and consequently, perhaps, a truer insight into, the type of character he sketches than Mr. Morrison. Mr. Pugh is kindly where Mr. Morrison is only caustic. . . . To Mr. Pugh's credit be it said, he selects for literary reproduction only such incidents as have in them something of pathos or of humour. Naturally enough, he sees little that is picturesque in Marsh Street, but when he does he seizes it like an artist."

The Pall Mall Budget.—"Mr. Pugh is subjective, and writes, in fact, professedly as one who had been brought up among the people he describes. He ranges over the fields of tragedy, and comedy, and farce . . . always with sympathy and intelligence. . . . The first sketch, 'The Courtship of Jack Cotter,' is genuinely humorous, and for pathos I would take 'Mamma's Angel.'"

The Manchester Guardian.—"All his characters live, move, and have their being, and we recognise a rare truthfulness to life in Hiram Sikes. 'A Street in Suburbia' has revealed Mr. Pugh's ability."

To-Day.—"Mr. Pugh has the gift of observation, the power of seeing those little things that make one man's character different from another. . . . Mr. Pugh can be genuinely funny when he chooses. The best thing in the book is 'The First and Last Meeting of the M.S.H.D.S.' The letters signify the 'Marsh Street Hall Debating Society.' If this were the only good thing in the book—which it isn't by a long way—it would still make the volume worth buying. . . . This is certainly one of the few books that ought to be bought, and not borrowed."

The Pioneer Series

VOL. VII.

The New Moon

By C. E. RAIMOND
Author of "George Mandeville's Husband"

The Daily Chronicle.—"In his new story, the author of 'George Mandeville's Husband' breaks fresh ground. . . . The satirical element in his former story was, no doubt, what made people talk about it, but it was not the finer portion of the work. . . . In 'The New Moon' no such element of attraction will be found. . . . It is a simple, poignant soul-drama, worked out entirely by three characters, a man and two women, one of whom remains to the last ignorant of the part she is playing. It may be said, perhaps, that there is a dash of satire in the portraiture of Millicent Monroe, with her childish, petulant, inconsequent mind, given over to the cult of signs and omens; but the character is delicately and sympathetically studied, without any touch of cruelty. Towards the end, indeed, this silver-grey figure becomes deeply pathetic, and may perhaps be regarded (whether the author so willed it or no) as the success of the book. It may appear . . . as though the book ought to be 'crowned' by the Thirteen Club, as works of edification are crowned by the French Academy. But we are not sure that the conclusion will be equally gratifying to that dare-devil body. If it does not actually justify the well-known superstition about 'seeing the new moon through glass,' it at least puts it to a symbolic use which the stalwart rationalism of the Thirteen Club will scarcely approve. Artistically, however, the symbolism is ingenious, subtle, and effective. The portrait of Dorothy Lance is as living as that of Millicent, though her characteristics are naturally less marked. . . . A story that moves us; and we must own to having read the last pages of 'The New Moon' with breathless interest and emotion."

The World.—"The plot of this story of a great friendship between a man and a woman is original and uncomplicated; the narration of it is simple, eloquent, and artistic; the tone is pure and poetical. There is a problem in it, but it is none the worse for that—no faint praise, surely."

The Daily News.—"It is a moving story, and in the supreme crisis it vibrates with restrained passion. The crisis is all the more impressive that the note of triumph and purity rings through its anguish."

The Saturday Review.—"The emotional phases are drawn with amazing force and sympathy. The book is a profoundly moving one, seizing hold of the reader from the very outset, and it makes a worthy member of what promises to be a very brilliant company of story-books indeed."

The Pioneer Series
VOL. VIII.

Milly's Story
(The New Moon)

By Mrs. MONTAGUE CRACKANTHORPE

The Pall Mall Gazette.—"'Milly's Story' seems to us a very clever account of a nervous, invalided woman, disposed by early education to be credulous, but possessed of a certain fine instinct with which wiser and duller people do not credit her."

The Daily Chronicle.—"There is a good deal of ingenuity in the way in which the incidents of the original tale are, so to speak, turned inside out."

The Liverpool Mercury.—"The nervous, sensitive, disease-stricken woman, hopelessly in love with a man who has given his heart to another, is a picture which will not easily fade from the mental vision."

The Saturday Review.—"In spite of our personal prejudice against the character, we must admit the story is a remarkably ingenious gloss upon Mr. Raimond's work. Indeed, the character is here far more convincing than it was in the original."

The Morning Post.—"Milly is not here quite the weakling, with a soul capable only of liberal credulity or timid fear. At moments she can hate, and the scene in which in imagination she places the naked truth before Dorothy's eyes is marked by honestly indignant passion."

The Realm.—"The author of 'Milly's Story' undertook a very difficult bit of work, and has carried it through with success. Milly's interview with the different occultists is very interesting reading, and satisfactorily explains many things in her life which were a puzzle. . . . 'Milly's Story' is very well written."

The Westminster Gazette.—"This is a clever book, and the descriptions of eminent palmists and other fashionable witches, which take up some portion of it, are a really interesting study of one most curious aspect of modern London life."

The World.—"The book is clever, curious, at times even pathetic."

Black and White.—"The point of view of the dabbler in occultism, who is neither a charlatan nor a frivolous pryer into secrets, has never been better put."

The Pioneer Series
VOL. IX.

Mrs Musgrave and Her Husband

By RICHARD MARSH.

The Times.—"Mr. Marsh's story is the extremely sensational romance of a double crime, and it is a decidedly original psychological study to boot. . . . The morality is perverse, and there is nothing of a moral, though the author may urge that he is not responsible for that. And morality apart, we can only say that we wish he had snatched the sinful couple from the police and continued their adventures through a second volume."

The National Observer.—"The interest is well sustained, and the book can be recommended as a good companion for a railway journey."

The St. James' Gazette.—"This is one of the completest things in the murder line we ever came across. De Quincey we know, and Miss Braddon, and Mr. William Shakespeare; all these on occasion have a pretty taste in blood. But compared with Mr. Richard Marsh, they are the merest amateurs."

The Daily Chronicle.—"Original and ingenious."

The Realm.—"The book is consistent, eminently readable, and told in a direct style."

The Daily Graphic.—"The best parts of the book are the psychological chapters, which are curious and original."

The Scotsman.—"An altogether interesting and excellently written story."

The Pall Mall Gazette.—"An exceedingly interesting tale."

Woman.—"A first-rate novel of sensation, tempered by some searching psychology."

Vanity Fair.—"The interest is absorbing from the first chapter, in which the keynote is artfully struck, to the logical climax."

The Manchester Guardian.—"The deadly duel between the two men in the Antwerp train, when the physical and moral contrast is admirably brought out, attains a very high level of dramatic power."

The Birmingham Gazette.—"With consummate skill Mr. Marsh sandwiches his horrors with exquisite bits of humour, and we lay down the book feeling that we have read an uncommonly clever novel."

The Pioneer Series

VOL. X.

The Red Badge of Courage

By STEPHEN CRANE

The Saturday Review.—"This extraordinary book will appeal strongly to the insatiable desire to know the psychology of war—how the sights and sounds, the terrible details of the drama of battle, affect the senses and the soul of man."

The Speaker.—"Every page is crowded, not merely with incidents such as the war correspondent describes, but with the tragedy of life. The reader sees the battle, not from afar, but from the inside. . . . As a work of art, 'The Red Badge of Courage' deserves high praise. As a moral lesson that mankind still needs, the praise it deserves is higher still."

The St. James' Gazette.—"This is not merely a remarkable book; it is a revelation. Mr. Crane has laid the War God on the dissecting-table and exposed his every bone and nerve and sinew and artery to the public gaze."

The Pall Mall Gazette.—"Mr. Crane has certainly written a remarkable book. He has deliberately synthesised the particular emotions of warfare, which, it is plain, he had been at pains to analyse fastidiously."

The Daily Chronicle.—"Mr. Kipling has shown us the private soldier in barrack and camp. Mr. Crane brings him into action. . . . Mr. Crane's book, we repeat, is a really fine achievement."

Black and White.—"Mr. Crane presents war, not in dramatic nor heroic aspect, but terrible and pitiful as it sometimes appears."

Mr. George Wyndham, M.P., in the **New Review.**—"Mr. Crane is a great artist. . . . In 'The Red Badge of Courage' he has surely contrived a masterpiece. . . . I think that his picture of war is more complete than Tolstoi's, more true than Zola's."

The Saturday Review (second notice).—"The curiosity of literary readers has been aroused by the extraordinary success of Mr. Stephen Crane, whose remarkable book, 'The Red Badge of Courage,' we reviewed in a recent issue. Mr. Crane is still a very young man, about twenty-three years of age. His book was written when he was twenty-one. . . . The extraordinary instance of early maturity is another proof of the fact that the imagination can enter into and realise the actualities of life so vividly and deeply as to surpass in realism the records of experience."

The Pioneer Series

VOL. XI.

The Demagogue and Lady Phayre

By W. J. LOCKE

Author of "At the Gate of Samaria"

The Daily Chronicle.—"Goddard and Lizzie, his wife, are both exceedingly well-drawn characters."

The Sketch.—"Mr. Locke's well-written, sensible, and sympathetic story."

The Scotsman.—"Not many stories of the kind are more cleverly written than this of Mr. Locke."

The Weekly Sun.—"Mr. Locke is a Realist, but a Realist in the best sense of the term. He has grappled with the soberest realities of everyday life, and rises triumphant from a contact that would be fatal to a writer of less splendid gifts."

The Yorkshire Herald.—"The story is worth reading, and is all the more entertaining because the hero's politics are not the theme of the book, but mere fragments of its inevitable embroidery."

The Liverpool Mercury.—"The characters of the story are drawn with a firm hand, and sad as many of them are, the details are eminently true to life."

Black and White.—"Contains admirable work."

The Sheffield Daily Telegraph.—"The story is cleverly written, with full knowledge of political life."

The Pioneer Series

VOL. XII.

Her Own Devices

BY C. G. COMPTON.

The Manchester Courier.—"Very bright and interesting."

The Daily Telegraph.—"Mr. Compton knows a good deal of theatrical and Bohemian society in London, and his pictures of it are forcible and realistic—the colours dashed on with careless skill. The book is full of cleverness.'

The Sketch.—"We are grateful to Mr. Compton for an entertaining book."

The Globe.—"The dialogue is bright throughout, and the tale makes very pleasant reading."

The Morning.—"The character of Susan Stanier is acutely observed, and in all her humours the actress—pushing, unscrupulous, vain, flighty, selfish creature that she is—is thoroughly human."

The Manchester Guardian.—"The author does not waste words in his descriptions, and he has not read his George Meredith in vain. Several of the characters are skilfully drawn."

In Preparation

Papier Mâché. By CHARLES ALLEN.

The New Virtue. By Mrs. OSCAR BERINGER.

Across an Ulster Bog. By M. HAMILTON.

One of God's Dilemmas. By ALLEN UPWARD.

The Novels of
Ivan Turgenev

TRANSLATED BY CONSTANCE GARNETT

Uniform Edition.   Post 8vo, cloth.   Price 3s. net each volume

The Times.—" A warm welcome, then, is due to the translations of Turgenev's novels, in course of publication by Mr. Heinemann."

The Daily Graphic.—" One cannot but be glad that Mr. Heinemann has thought fit to produce a satisfactory little edition of the exquisitely pathetic tales of Turgenev."

VOL. I.
Rudin

The Pall Mall Gazette.—" The method is perfect; difficulties of character overcome without explanation, subtleties so objectively brought out in conversation, for instance—that we might almost fancy the author himself did not know how much he was saying—a simplicity which apparently only Russian novelists possess."

VOL. II.
A House of Gentlefolk

The Times.—" Readers may content themselves with admiring 'A House of Gentlefolk' for those beauties which belong to all ages and countries."

VOL. III.
On the Eve

The Scotsman.—" The work has a thousand good qualities, the best of which defy analysis, but will charm any one who reads the story."

The Literary World.—" It is human nature between two covers, a simple tale told simply by a genius."

The Novels of Ivan Turgenev
(*Continued*)

VOL. IV.
Fathers and Children

The Realm.—"The supreme excellence of the book consists in the fact that it possesses merits which are rarely found in combination. It is at once a great work of art and a profound study of a movement. . . . The book abounds in passages of idyllic beauty far too numerous to quote."

The Scotsman.—"Bazaroo is a type of modern scepticism, and the art of the story consists in the skill with which this type is brought into contrast with other types and temperaments."

VOLS. VII. AND VIII.
A Sportsman's Sketches
IN 2 VOLS.

The Times.—"It is superfluous to praise the excellent tales of Turgenev—'A Sportsman's Sketches.' The strong, unaffected, and sympathetic drawing of rustic character, the landscape, the very atmosphere, are all alike admirable."

The Daily Chronicle.—"The great Russian has no cleverness, no violence, no mannerism, but he has the rare beauty of patient and peaceful art. Terrible wisdom and insight are his, infinite emotion not suffered to be lawless, immense strength adorned with delicacy and grace, and at heart that necessary of artists—a boundless devotion to his own land, which has inspired him to his great achievements. His work is compassionate, beautiful, unique; in the sight of fellow-craftsmen always marvellous and often perfect."

VOL. V.
Smoke

VOLS. VI. AND VII.
Virgin Soil

The Novels of Björnstjerne Björnson

Edited by Edmund Gosse

Uniform Edition. Post 8vo, cloth. 3s. net per volume

The Literary World.—" The excellent edition of Björnson."

VOL. I.
Synnové Solbakken

The Literary World.—" We are shown in the course of a book which is almost devoid of plot the peasant at work, in love, and at fisticuffs; but the simpler the page the more prominent the genius of a writer who, asking no help from the novelist, touches the common with the magic of his power till the result is a whole that enchants."

VOL. II.
Arne

The Academy.—" This tale of the peasant-poet who 'went on tending the cattle and making songs,' while he was 'shy of all whom he did not know, and disliked them because he believed they disliked him,' has all the simple and poetical charm of Björnson's best works, and contains some of his best lyrics."

VOL. III.
A Happy Boy

VOL. IV.
The Fisher Maiden

VOL. V.
The Bridal March

VOL. VI.
Magnhild

VOL. VII.
Captain Mansana

LONDON: WILLIAM HEINEMANN
21 BEDFORD STREET, W.C.

www.ingramcontent.com/pod-product-compliance
Lightning Source LLC
Chambersburg PA
CBHW020907230426
43666CB00008B/1344